Complete Conditioning
for Martial Arts

Sean Cochran

Human Kinetics

Library of Congress Cataloging-in-Publication Data

Cochran, Sean, 1971-
  Complete conditioning for martial arts / Sean Cochran.
    p. cm.
    ISBN 0-7360-0250-2
      1. Martial arts--Training. I. Title.

GV1102.7.T7C63 2001

613.7'148--dc21   00-054017

ISBN: 0-7360-0250-2

Copyright © 2001 by Sean Cochran

Developmental Editor: Kent Reel; **Managing Editor:** Cynthia McEntire; **Assistant Editors:** Kim Thoren and John Wentworth; **Copyeditor:** Jan Feeney; **Proofreader:** Coree Schutter; **Permission Manager:** Toni Harte; **Graphic Designer:** Stuart Cartwright; **Graphic Artist:** Dody Bullerman; **Photo Manager:** Tom Roberts; **Cover Designer:** Jack W. Davis; **Photographer (cover):** © Ray Malace; **Photographer (interior):** Tom Roberts; **Printer:** United Graphics

Human Kinetics books are available at special discounts for bulk purchase. Special editions or book excerpts can also be created to specification. For details, contact the Special Sales Manager at Human Kinetics.

Printed in the United States of America   10 9 8 7 6 5 4 3 2 1

Human Kinetics
Web site: www.humankinetics.com

United States: Human Kinetics
P.O. Box 5076
Champaign, IL 61825-5076
800-747-4457
e-mail: humank@hkusa.com

Canada: Human Kinetics
475 Devonshire Road Unit 100
Windsor, ON N8Y 2L5
800-465-7301 (in Canada only)
e-mail: orders@hkcanada.com

Europe: Human Kinetics
Units C2/C3 Wira Business Park
West Park Ring Road
Leeds LS16 6EB, United Kingdom
+44 (0) 113 278 1708
e-mail: hk@hkeurope.com

Australia: Human Kinetics
57A Price Avenue
Lower Mitcham, South
Australia 5062
08 8277 1555
e-mail: liahka@senet.com.au

New Zealand: Human Kinetics
P.O. Box 105-231, Auckland
Central
09-523-3462
e-mail: hkp@ihug.co.nz

This book is dedicated to Dr. Tom House and Mustapha Abdul-Jalil. Special thanks go to Tammy Wright, Gina Modelo, and the staff at the San Diego Taekwon-Do Center.

CONTENTS

INTRODUCTION

Complete Conditioning for Martial Arts provides a solid foundation of the necessary requirements for optimal performance in the martial arts and illustrates over 80 exercises to help increase your strength, flexibility, endurance, and power.

Chapter 1 reviews the physical parameters involved in the martial arts and how these parameters apply to your martial art. This chapter also covers essential information about fitness. In chapter 2, you will learn to evaluate your current fitness level and identify your strengths and weaknesses.

Chapters 3, 4, and 5 present programs and exercises that develop flexibility, joint stability, and torso stability, which make up the basic foundation of martial arts training. You cannot improve in your martial art if you lack flexibility, joint stability, and torso stability. These three elements fulfill two primary needs of any martial artist: function and injury prevention.

Whether you are competing in the Olympics or just practicing kicks in the backyard, you need a certain level of strength, flexibility, endurance, and muscular balance to function at your best. If you do not have the required levels of strength, flexibility, endurance, or balance, you won't be able to perform biomechanical movements correctly. You will also be more vulnerable to injury. The risk of injury increases with participation in the martial arts, regardless of the martial arts technique. If your body does not have the resilience in its bones, ligaments, and muscles, an injury will occur. Exercises for flexibility, joint stabilization, and torso stabilization help prevent injuries. Chapters 3, 4, and 5 cover the essence of what you need to develop a strong foundation.

The focus of this book is performance improvement. A complete martial arts training program should be geared toward total body improvement in all areas of importance—flexibility, strength, endurance, aerobic and anaerobic output, speed, and agility. The main goal of this book is to improve performance in all these areas. The foundation you will develop through using chapters 3, 4, and 5 will help you enhance performance. Function and injury prevention must be addressed first, through specific exercises, or your strides toward optimal performance in the martial arts will be significantly hindered.

As chapters 3, 4, and 5 focus on developing a strong base for your training program, chapters 6 and 7 aim at improving physical performance. The exercises in these chapters expand your muscular strength, endurance, speed, agility, and power. Directions for all the core and plyometric exercises, both on machines and with free weights, are explained in detail and shown in photos. While these exercises do improve integrative functioning and reduce injury risk, their main purpose is enhanced performance. (By contrast, while the exercises in chapters 3 through 5 do enhance performance, their chief aim is to improve integrative functioning and reduce injury risk.)

Chapter 8 deals with increasing aerobic and anaerobic output and improving speed and agility. In chapter 9, we look at recovery and nutrition. Finally, in chapter 10, you will learn how to put it all together to create a workout tuned to your goals and the requirements of your martial art.

CHAPTER 1

FITNESS ESSENTIALS

The martial arts have been around for centuries, evolving into many different styles along the way, each with its own focus and philosophy. This first chapter provides an overview of the different styles and physical requirements of many of the martial arts practiced throughout the world. The chapter also covers the fitness essentials of martial arts training, principles of conditioning, and some of the differences among the disciplines grouped under the umbrella term *martial arts*.

DISCIPLINES WITHIN THE MARTIAL ARTS

The following is a list of many of the commonly practiced martial arts, each with a definition and a brief summary. Review this list to understand the many different styles and physical requirements of the martial arts. This is not a comprehensive list of all the martial arts in the world; it is only a summary.

• **Aikido:** A Japanese martial art that focuses on redirecting an opponent's energy, Aikido involves the use of many joint locks and techniques focused on controlling the attacker. *Aikido* means "the way of the harmonious spirit."

• **Jujitsu:** This is another martial art that developed in Japan. Many hand techniques and striking attacks are prevalent, as well as grappling and throwing techniques. Little emphasis is placed on the development of flexibility or aerobic conditioning throughout its training system. *Jujitsu* is defined as "the soft method."

• **Judo:** An Olympic sport that originated in Japan, Judo focuses on throws. "Throws" refer to grappling techniques that actually flip the opponent onto the ground. The physical nature of this art is extreme, requiring large amounts of strength, power, and endurance.

• **Karate:** Developed in Okinawa, Japan, Karate uses a variety of lower- and upper-body defensive and offensive moves. Karate requires flexibility, balance, strength, and aerobic conditioning for optimal performance. *Karate* is defined as "empty hand."

• **Kung fu:** Originating in China, this martial art focuses on kicks and punches, with a secondary emphasis on balance. Kung fu is a physically rigorous martial art requiring a high level of fitness. *Kung fu* is defined as "skill" or "art."

• **Muay thai:** A martial art that originated in Thailand, Muay thai provides its practitioners with full-contact sparring and full-contact matches. This physically rigorous martial art often requires students to perform activities such as shadow boxing, heavy bag work, sparring, and jumping rope.

• **Taekwondo:** A Korean martial art that develops the skills of *punching and kicking*, Taekwondo's major emphasis is on foot techniques. Taekwondo requires flexibility, muscular strength, and power. *Taekwondo* is defined as "the art of the hand and foot."

This list is just a sample of the many martial arts that exist and the physical requirements of them. There are many other martial arts that are pleasant and produce physical and mental benefits. Table 1.1 lists martial arts styles and the physical requirements of each style. The physical classifications are aerobic level, anaerobic level, flexibility, muscular strength, and muscular power. Use this table as a guide for the physical requirements of the martial art you currently practice or are planning to study.

Table 1.1   Physical Requirements for Selected Martial Arts

Martial art	Aerobic level	Anaerobic level	Flexibility	Muscular strength	Muscular power
Aikido	Low	Low	Moderate	Moderate	Low
Jujitsu	Low	Low	Moderate	Moderate	Moderate
Judo	High	High	Moderate	High	High
Karate	High	High	High	Moderate	High
Kung fu	High	High	High	Moderate	High
Muay thai	High	Moderate	Moderate	Moderate	High
Taekwondo	High	High	High	Moderate	High

Each martial art requires its own set of physical attributes for success and enjoyment. Remember: no martial art is better than another—just different.

PHYSICAL QUALITIES

Now that you have a basic understanding of some of the different styles of martial arts and their physical requirements, let's discuss how to use this book. Our focus is on developing the physical qualities to participate and excel in the martial arts. We will look at what is required of your body in terms of aerobic conditioning, anaerobic conditioning, muscular strength, flexibility, and power. We will list exercises in all these categories and discuss program design and setup. Before we move to all this information, let's review the basic athletic requirements for the martial arts.

Muscular Strength

Muscular strength is the amount of force that a muscle or muscles can exert against an outside source of resistance in one maximal effort. The muscles in your body contract and relax to perform skeletal movement. When you walk, you ask muscles in your lower extremities to contract and relax in a sequential order to perform this skeletal movement. In the martial arts, when you throw a punch, your body performs a sequential order of muscle contractions to move your fist.

The bench press is an example of muscular strength in resistance training. The amount of muscular strength in the upper body determines the amount of weight you can lift in this exercise. For example, a person able to lift 240 pounds for five repetitions at the beginning of a weightlifting program may improve after three months to lift 250 pounds for five repetitions. By increasing the amount of weight lifted over time, the person has improved muscle strength.

Improved muscular strength directly correlates to improvement in the martial arts. Judo, for example, requires muscular strength. After developing or improving your base of muscular strength, you will be able to perform judo techniques with greater ease. You will become less fatigued, improve your technique, and see an overall improvement in the art. We will discuss resistance-training techniques and protocols in greater depth in later chapters.

Now that you understand muscular strength, we will move on to the next athletic requirement: muscular power.

Muscular Power

Muscular power is another factor necessary for optimal performance in the martial arts. Muscular movements in the body can occur at different rates. A muscle in your system can contract at a rapid rate or at a very slow rate. For example, if you were practicing a certain kick on the heavy bag, you would attempt to hit the bag as quickly as possible with each kick. You would not want to kick the bag slowly because you would execute the kick incorrectly. The body also can contract a muscle very slowly. When you lift a very heavy weight, your body may require a very slow contraction of the muscle to lift the load. The point is that many movements in the martial arts require a quick, explosive contraction of a muscle or muscles. This requires the development of muscular power.

Muscular power is the development of force within a muscle or muscles in the shortest amount of time possible. By developing muscular power, you strive to perform specific muscular actions in the shortest amount of time. For example, the execution of a side kick in karate is more effective in competition if you are able to execute the entire kick, start to finish, in .03 second rather than .05 second. It's easy to see that the execution of a certain technique is more effective when done in a shorter amount of time.

The other factor concerning muscular power is force development. The development of power involves the process of developing force. The development of force coincides with muscular strength. Power and force development are similar in that both are concerned with the development of muscular force; the difference is that power has a regard for time. Muscular power involves developing muscular force in the shortest time possible. A compromise in the development of force to enhance the speed of a movement is not the desired result when you train for muscular power. The desired result is actually an increase in both force and speed.

As an example, consider that side kick again. It would be to your advantage to train to increase your muscular power, improve the speed of your side kick, and increase the force behind the kick. The benefits of training for muscular power are evident.

Muscular Endurance

The third relevant term is muscular endurance. Muscular endurance is the ability of a muscle or muscles to repeatedly perform muscular contractions over an extended period of time. When you practice or participate in a martial arts competition, you are required to perform certain movements repeatedly. For example, if you were in a sparring competition that consisted of five two-minute rounds, you would have to repeat many movements several times with little or no rest between movements. This type of situation requires a certain stamina of the muscular system, known as muscular endurance.

Performing repeated muscular actions over time causes fatigue within the muscular system. As a result, muscular performance decreases. To prevent such a scenario from occurring during a martial arts competition or practice session, you need to develop endurance so that muscular fatigue doesn't prevent you from performing techniques correctly and efficiently. Training for muscular endurance will result in a high level of resistance to fatigue by your muscular system.

Muscular Balance

For every action performed by a muscle, another muscle must reverse or slow down this action. For example, when you throw a punch in karate, certain muscle groups extend your hand outward. To complete the technique, a second muscle group slows down and reverses the action. The amount of muscular power, strength, and endurance required to extend the punch needs to be equal in both sets of muscles. If you do not have balance between these two opposing muscle groups, one group will experience a greater amount of stress, which results in greater fatigue, lower performance output, and a higher risk of injury. Your training should focus on creating a balance in opposing muscle groups' strength, power, and endurance.

Aerobic Power

Aerobic power involves the efficiency with which your body fuels its systems with oxygen. It is usually measured by the rate of efficiency that oxygen is used by working muscles. Many martial arts require long bouts of continuous physical movement without rest. For example, when performing a series of katas in a row or going through a series of sparring rounds, you ask your body to work for an extended period with no rest. Your muscles require oxygen and nutrients to continue functioning at a high level. If your body is efficient in delivering oxygen to your working muscles, it will be able to perform at a high level for a long time.

Anaerobic Power

Anaerobic power concerns the amount of work a person performs during physical activities, similar to aerobic power. The difference is that anaerobic power is the rate of efficiency at which work is performed *without oxygen*. When you perform rapid, powerful muscle contractions in a short amount of time, your body is not able to supply muscles with oxygen to perform these actions. Your muscles have to use energy already stored in them at the time of these muscular activities.

For example, a roundhouse kick in taekwondo is very quick and powerful. You want to perform this kick as quickly as possible to increase the possibility of scoring a point. When you perform this kick, the contractions in your muscular system are very quick. A great amount of muscular power is created in a very short time. This results in a series of muscular contractions occurring in the absence of oxygen.

This example gives you a good understanding of the importance of increasing the anaerobic thresholds within your muscular and cardio-respiratory systems. Doing so allows for more efficient execution of powerful, rapid techniques over a greater period of time.

Muscular Flexibility

Muscular flexibility refers to the range of motion (ROM) around a joint. A joint is the place where bones meet. Joints are usually cushioned by a type of cartilage. Fibrous attachments known as tendons attach muscles to bones and hold joints together. Muscles create movement in the joints through their contractions. This action translates into skeletal movements.

Any movement in the martial arts requires skeletal actions and joint movements. Some techniques require a large range of motion in certain joints. For example, a turning hook kick in taekwondo requires a wide range of motion in the hip joint. This technique is very difficult for a person with a low range of motion in the hip joint. Since many martial arts techniques require a wide range of motion in the joints, you should include a flexibility program in your conditioning program. Chapter 3 deals with flexibility work and the benefits of a flexibility program.

Speed

Speed is the rapidity of movement. Any muscular action can be measured in terms of speed. A common test for speed is the 50-yard dash. The faster you can run 50 yards, the more success you will have in an athletic event that requires speed in such distances. The crossover to the martial arts is easy to make. The faster you can perform a certain technique, the more you can improve that technique. For example, during a sparring competition if you perform a side kick in .05 second, your opponent may be able to block the kick. The kick was too slow to be successful. If you can perform the side kick in .03 second, your opponent may be unable to block the kick, and you would score a point.

The development and improvement of speed is a result of combining a few variables. Improvement in the execution of techniques is one facet. You will not improve the speed of a kick if your technique is incorrect. Improvement in muscular strength, power, flexibility, and proper technique will result in an improvement in speed.

Agility

Agility is the ability to rapidly change direction of the body or body parts *under control*. An example is the ability to cut on the basketball court. This movement requires an abrupt change of direction while controlling the ball and your body.

Many of the martial arts require agility. For example, in judo if you are squared shoulder to shoulder with your opponent and want to flip him or her over your back, you will need to quickly shift your body into the correct position to complete the throw.

ENERGY SYSTEMS

Your body is fueled by adenosine triphosphate (ATP), which is delivered via three systems: the phosphagen system, glycolytic system, and oxidative system. The phosphagen system fuels the body for short, intense bouts of muscular actions without oxygen (anaerobic exercise). The glycolytic system is divided into fast and slow glycolysis. Fast glycolysis fuels the muscles with limited oxygen and uses stored glycogen to produce ATP. Slow glycolysis uses larger amounts of oxygen and glycogen to fuel muscles for activities that last longer than 30 seconds. The oxidative system kicks in after approximately two minutes of activity and uses carbohydrates and fats with oxygen for the production of ATP (aerobic exercise). This information helps you determine which energy systems are used in your martial art and allows you to design your training program to enhance these energy systems.

Table 1.2 lists durations of activity and types of energy systems used during physical activity. As you can see in the table, each energy system has a specified time frame in which it is used and an intensity level that uses each energy system. The roundhouse kick, for example, is an activity of very high intensity that uses the phosphagen system. If the intensity of an activity is very low, neither the phosphagen system nor fast glycolysis will be used. It is imperative to know which energy systems you use in your martial art. Your training outside the studio will specifically train your body to be more efficient in the production and replenishment of ATP from a specific energy system. For example, if you find that your martial art requires short, very intense activities, you will want to train your phosphagen and fast glycolytic systems. On the other hand, if your activities are less intense but are of long duration, you would want to focus your training on developing the efficiency of your oxidative system.

Table 1.2   Energy System Usage Chart

Duration of activity	Intensity of activity	Energy system used	Example in martial arts
0–6 sec	Very high intensity	Phosphagen	Roundhouse kick in taekwondo
6–30 sec	High intensity	Fast glycolysis	Series of side kicks
30 sec–2 min	Moderate intensity	Slow glycolysis	When feeling the "burn" after a prolonged series of side kicks
Greater than 2 min	Low intensity	Oxidative	Practicing katas for 2 hours

Another important point is that when your muscles receive a rest period, a recovery process occurs that replenishes the ATP stores in your system. When you actively train your body, it becomes more efficient in its delivery system and replenishment of energy stores. That is why it is necessary to train specifically to the energy system you use in your martial art. Some of the martial arts use all three systems, while others use predominantly one system. Before you begin training, determine what energy system or systems your martial art uses.

TRAINING PRINCIPLES

The following information on training principles gives you a base of knowledge to help you individualize your training program to the needs of your martial art. When reading through these principles, keep in mind that they all work together to benefit your training. The training principles are adaptation, overload, specificity training, and periodization.

Adaptation

The adaptation principle is the body's ability to adapt to the demands placed on it by external stimuli. This principle is the basis for all resistance training. For your body to improve in strength, power, flexibility, or speed, you must provide sufficient stimuli. For example, when you lift heavier weights than your body is used to on a daily basis, your body will adapt by becoming stronger. To develop quicker kicks, you must provide a stimulus to create the necessary adaptation.

Overload

The overload principle states that the human body will adapt to the increased resistance placed on it by becoming stronger, faster, or more conditioned. To improve muscular strength, power, flexibility, or endurance, you need to stress the body beyond what it has experienced before. In response to the increased stress, your body compensates, causing it to adapt to the external stimuli.

For example, to improve upper-body strength using resistance training, increase the load (weight) in your upper-body resistance training to cause an improvement in your strength. For any physical improvement, it is necessary to place an overload on the system. If you need to improve the muscular strength of your lower body for the purpose of kicking, you will need to place an overload on your lower body.

The next principle, specificity training, encompasses both adaptation and overload.

Specificity Training

Specificity training refers to the similarity between a training activity and a sport. You must choose training drills and exercises that simulate your martial art and are specific to your desired outcomes. In a judo match, certain physical movements have to occur for you to flip your opponent. When you attempt a turning heel kick in taekwondo, your body follows a certain neuromuscular pattern to perform the kick. For your body to become better and more efficient at any physical movement, you need to train the body through the motions of that movement. For example, when training for a marathon, a runner may include several long training runs. This prepares the runner's body for the rigors of the marathon. If you are attempting to develop greater punching power, your resistance training should focus on exercises that develop power in the shoulder and arm muscles.

Periodization

Many athletes use periodization to plan their training, and this principle is almost always an integral part of any training program. Periodization is the cycling of loads, volumes, intensity, and exercises within a given time period. The time frame may be divided into days, weeks, months, or even years. Further, the changes in load, volume, and intensity in each cycle help prevent overtraining while still allowing optimal gains in muscular strength, endurance, and power. Periodization is discussed in greater detail in chapter 10.

LOAD, VOLUME, DURATION, AND FREQUENCY: PUTTING IT ALL TOGETHER

Frequency is how often a specific exercise or set of exercises are performed within a given amount of time. For example, if you perform power cleans for overall power development twice a week, a specified frequency of this exercise has occurred, which translates into a certain level of intensity. If you do power cleans three times in the following week, you have increased your intensity level for this exercise by performing it at a greater frequency in the same time frame. This is a good example of how intensity, load, volume, duration, and frequency function together to develop a certain level of training intensity.

Different intensity levels of training will train your neuromuscular system for different adaptations. The four variables—load, volume, duration, and frequency—can be manipulated together or as separate entities to create a particular intensity level in your training. Let's take a closer look at these variables.

Different repetition levels result in different training outcomes. Repetition and load (percent of 1-repetition maximum) are linked. High-repetition sets are coupled with low intensities and large volumes to increase muscular endurance. This is a prime example of how adjusting two variables results in a particular training intensity and creates a certain training outcome. This type of repetition and load assignment is ideal for a martial artist attempting to increase muscular endurance and reduce fatigue when training.

A few other examples should give you a good understanding of this concept. A martial artist who needs increased muscular strength would use moderate repetition, moderate intensity, and moderate volume to achieve such results. A martial artist interested in training for both strength and speed would use low repetition, high intensity, and low volume. Varying repetition levels, volumes, and loads results in differing intensity levels to achieve improved muscular strength and movement speed. Remember that different intensity levels result in different training outcomes. See table 1.3 for details on the integration of training types and training variables.

Always remember this: these variables can be modified as a group or individually. To increase the overall intensity of your workout, for

Table 1.3   Integrating Training Types and Training Variables

Type of training	Load and intensity	Repetitions per set	Time between sets	Workout frequency
Strength/ hypertrophy	70–90%	6–12	30–60 sec	4 times per week
Endurance	70% and below	15 and greater	60 sec or less	2–6 times per week
Power	90% and greater	5 and below	2–3 min	2–3 times per week
Balance	90% and below	6 and greater	2 min or less	2–6 times per week

example, you could increase the load of each set or increase both the load and intensity of each exercise.

Before moving on, you need to understand each variable and determine how it comes into play when training for muscular strength, endurance, power, and balance. Review the information about muscular strength, endurance, and power. This quick review will give you a good idea of the requirements for improvements in each area. Once you have an understanding of the classifications of muscular strength, endurance, and power, you will be able to properly adjust these variables to your benefit.

Finally, you'll note that one of the training variables—volume—is not shown in table 1.3. Volume is a dependent variable. Volume is a function of load, intensity, repetitions, sets, and workout frequency. Remember, volume refers to the total amount of weight lifted in a given training session or sessions. Volume is also defined as the total number of repetitions and the varying loads lifted within a training session. Volume is the weight × the number of repetitions × the sets performed in a given exercise. For example, if you bench press 200 pounds for 10 repetitions in three sets, the total volume for that exercise would be

$$200 \times 10 \times 3 = 6{,}000 \text{ pounds.}$$

There is an inverse relationship between intensity and volume. When the intensity or load is high in a training regimen, the total volume of that training session will be low. When intensity or load is low, total volume will be high.

SUMMARY

This chapter contains a great deal of information. Let's put it all together so that you have a solid understanding before moving on.

Three energy systems—phosphagen, glycolytic, and oxidative—provide fuel during physical activity. The important thing to remember is which energy system fuels your body. This depends on two conditions: the length of physical activity and the intensity level. Review the physical requirements of your martial art and train to enhance the energy system that provides your body with fuel during your training.

The principles of specificity, adaptation, and overload influence martial arts training. To enhance your performance in your martial art, match your training to the neuromuscular movements in your specific martial arts discipline. To allow for a crossover effect to occur, you must match your resistance-training exercises to the movements in your martial art. Performance specificity in your training is necessary. The body adapts to the stresses placed on it, so for improvement in physical performance your body requires a stimulus that gradually places greater stress on your body (adaptation). This is also where overload comes into play. An overload on your neuromuscular system must occur on a continuum for the principle of adaptation to result. You have to continually place greater stress on your body for improvements in physical performance. The overload placed on your body in your resistance training must be specific for an improvement in your martial art to occur.

Let's review intensity. Remember, the intensity level of your resistance training has a direct correlation to the muscular adaptations your body makes. A quick review of table 1.3 shows you that differing intensity levels result in distinct adaptations by your neuromuscular system in the areas of muscular power, strength, endurance, and balance. The training variables of load, volume, duration, and frequency can be altered as a group or as individual variables to increase or decrease the intensity level of your training. Be specific in terms of your intensity level of training and predetermined training goals.

One last point to remember about these training variables is the inverse relationship between volume and intensity. Volume is a combination of repetitions and sets per workout. When you train at a high intensity (greater than 90 percent), your total training volume is low. On the other hand, when intensity is low (less than 65 percent), your overall training volume is high.

Use all of the information in this chapter to individualize your training to meet the specific requirements of your martial art. Be specific in the areas you need to develop, such as muscular endurance. Train to improve the energy system that predominantly fuels your body during your martial art. Use the principles of specificity, adaptation, and overload to receive the greatest benefit from your training. Adjust the training variables (load, volume, duration, and frequency) to match the desired level of training intensity. Finally, use a periodization schedule that allows you to focus on particular variables within a certain time frame.

CHAPTER 2

FITNESS EVALUATION

Fitness testing involves conducting individual tests to assess a person's ability to perform specific physical activities. Test results will help you identify areas of strength and weakness in your physical makeup. Fitness testing also functions as a screening for any possible health risks. One point to remember about these tests is that they measure individual abilities. The results of your tests are not a measuring stick to compare against other students or friends; they are simply useful tools to help you improve your skills in the martial arts.

The tests in this chapter will give you a starting point for your training. These tests cover each performance category discussed in chapter 1: muscular strength, muscular power, endurance, flexibility, aerobic output, anaerobic output, speed, and agility. A set of testing guidelines also is included, with an advisable procedure for setup, implementation, and recording.

TESTING PROCEDURES

Proper execution of each test ensures safety and accurate results. First you should find a friend or classmate to help you set up, measure, and record the results from these tests, as it is difficult to test yourself and record a valid score at the same time.

Once you have found a partner to assist you, the process becomes quite simple. Follow the instructions and record your results. Do the tests in order for one important reason: portions of the test will result in a high level of muscular fatigue. It is necessary to perform tests requiring high levels of coordination first; otherwise, fatigue will skew the results of these tests.

One more piece of advice: allow three to five minutes of rest between each test to allow your body to recover fully. If you do not allow any recovery time, some of the tests will not be accurate because you'll be fatigued. Tests that require more than one trial also specify the amount of rest allowed between each trial.

Equipment

Table 2.1 lists the equipment needed to perform each test properly. The use of proper equipment will enhance the validity and reliability of each test.

As you can see, very little equipment is needed to give you a base set of recordings to begin your testing. Before we map out the specific tests, let's look at a few points to keep in mind throughout your testing.

Guidelines

You should complete this series of tests before beginning your new training program. The first set of test results should be recorded with a date. These results will be your baseline series. The baseline series will give you the information to determine where you need to improve in your physical conditioning. For example, if you scored low in the category of muscular strength, your next training program should emphasize muscular strength.

You should retest yourself at given intervals throughout your training. You set your own intervals. It is recommended that you perform a second set of tests after a specified amount of training or immediately after a competition. This will allow you to follow up your baseline test

Table 2.1   Equipment Needed for Fitness Testing

Fitness parameter	Practical test	Required equipment
Muscular strength	10-rep maximum	Free weights
Muscular power	Squat jump Power push-up	Stopwatch Stopwatch, medicine ball
Aerobic power	2-mile run 3-min step test	Stopwatch, running track Stopwatch, 12-inch box
Anaerobic power	Line drill Shuttle run	Stopwatch, running track, cones Stopwatch, running track, cones
Speed	20-yard dash	Stopwatch, running track
Agility	T-test Edgren side step	Stopwatch, cones Stopwatch, tape
Flexibility	Sit and reach	Sit-and-reach box

results with additional information that will tell you if your training has been beneficial in the weak areas.

A good interval time to retest is every three to six months. This amount of time allows your training program to develop some results. If you find that you made few gains in certain areas, then it is a good idea to change some variable in your next training program segment. If the second series of tests shows improvements, then you will not need to change much for your next training segment.

Remember that these tests help you determine if the training programs you have in place are properly adjusted to improve your results in each test. Keeping a journal in which you record all your test results allows you to review all of your tests at the same time. Now let's move to the specific instructions for each test.

Testing Protocol

Following is a series of tests that provide you with a large base of information on your levels of muscular strength, power, endurance, flexibility, aerobic output, anaerobic output, speed, and agility. Before you begin testing, perform a proper warm-up consisting of a five-minute aerobic activity (such as jogging or cycling), flexibility work, and some low-intensity anaerobic drills.

Many of the fitness tests in this chapter are adapted, by permission, from *Essentials of Strength Training and Conditioning*, 2nd ed., by NSCA, edited by Thomas R. Baechle and Roger W. Earle, copyright 2000, Human Kinetics, Champaign, IL.

10-REPETITION MAXIMUM

You will use your 1-repetition maximum (1RM) to set the intensity level of your resistance training. Your 1RM refers to the number of reps that your can perform with a load versus the most weight you can lift once. Chapter 10 goes into further detail about how to use your 1RM to create your resistance program. This test will help you determine your 1RM based on your 10-repetition maximum. You will need a set of free weights and a spotter. (Regardless of your skill level, always use a spotter!) Also, an experienced instructor can help find your 10-repetition maximum in fewer than five trials.

Procedure

1. If you are new to resistance training, begin with a lighter weight.

2. Perform a set of 10 repetitions with the light weight.

3. Rest two to four minutes between sets.

4. For the second set, add additional weight based on the ease with which you completed the first set. For example, if you easily lifted 225 pounds for 10 repetitions, the next increment would be large. On the other hand, if your 225-pound lift was difficult but you completed 10 repetitions, your next raise in weight would be small.

5. Perform another set of 10 repetitions.

6. Continue the process of performing 10 repetitions, resting, and adding weight until you discover a weight that allows only 10 repetitions. This is your 10-repetition maximum. Check table 2.2 to find your 1RM based on your 10-repetition maximum.

Table 2.2 Determining 1-Repetition Maximum

% of 1RM	100.0	93.5	91.0	88.5	86.0	83.5	81.0	78.5	76.0	73.5
Repetitions	**1**	**2**	**3**	**4**	**5**	**6**	**7**	**8**	**9**	**10**
Weight lifted	0.0	0.0	0.0	0.0	0.0	0.0	0.0	0.0	0.0	0.0
(lbs)	5.0	4.7	4.5	4.4	4.3	4.2	4.1	3.9	3.8	3.7
	10.0	9.4	9.1	8.9	8.6	8.4	8.2	7.9	7.6	7.4
	15.0	14.0	13.7	13.3	12.9	12.5	12.2	11.8	11.4	11.0
	20.0	18.7	18.2	17.7	17.2	16.7	16.2	15.7	15.2	14.7
	25.0	23.4	22.8	22.1	21.5	20.9	20.2	19.6	19.0	18.4
	30.0	28.1	27.3	26.6	25.8	25.1	24.3	23.6	22.8	22.1
	35.0	32.7	31.9	31.0	30.1	29.2	28.4	27.5	26.6	25.7
	40.0	37.4	36.4	35.4	34.4	33.4	32.4	31.4	30.4	29.4
	45.0	42.1	41.0	39.8	38.7	37.6	36.5	35.3	34.2	33.1
	50.0	46.8	45.5	44.3	43.0	41.8	40.5	39.3	38.0	36.8
	55.0	51.4	50.1	48.7	47.3	45.9	44.6	43.2	41.8	40.4
	60.0	56.1	54.6	53.1	51.6	50.1	48.6	47.1	45.6	44.1
	65.0	60.8	59.2	57.5	55.9	54.3	52.7	51.0	49.4	47.8
	70.0	65.5	63.7	62.0	60.2	58.5	56.7	55.0	53.2	51.5
	75.0	70.1	68.3	66.4	64.5	62.6	60.8	58.9	57.0	55.1
	80.0	74.8	72.8	70.8	68.8	66.8	64.8	62.8	60.8	58.8
	85.0	79.5	77.4	75.2	73.1	71.0	68.9	66.7	64.6	62.5
	90.0	84.2	81.9	79.7	77.4	75.2	72.9	70.7	68.4	66.2
	95.0	88.8	86.5	84.1	81.7	79.3	77.0	74.6	72.2	69.8
	100.0	93.5	91.0	88.5	86.0	83.5	81.0	78.5	76.0	73.5
	105.0	98.2	95.6	92.9	90.3	87.7	85.1	82.4	79.8	77.2
	110.0	102.9	100.1	97.4	94.6	91.9	89.1	86.4	83.6	80.9
	115.0	107.5	104.7	101.8	98.9	96.0	93.2	90.3	87.4	84.5
	120.0	112.2	109.2	106.2	103.2	100.2	97.2	94.2	91.2	88.2
	125.0	116.9	113.8	110.6	107.5	104.4	101.3	98.1	95.0	91.9
	130.0	121.6	118.3	115.1	111.8	108.6	105.3	102.1	98.8	95.6
	135.0	126.2	122.9	119.5	116.1	112.7	109.4	106.0	102.6	99.2
	140.0	130.9	127.4	123.9	120.4	116.9	113.4	109.9	106.4	102.9
	145.0	135.6	132.0	128.3	124.7	121.1	117.5	113.8	110.2	106.6
	150.0	140.3	136.5	132.8	129.0	125.3	121.5	117.8	114.0	110.3
	155.0	144.9	141.1	137.2	133.3	129.4	125.6	121.7	117.8	113.9
	160.0	149.6	145.6	141.6	137.6	133.6	129.6	125.6	121.6	117.6
	165.0	154.3	150.2	146.0	141.9	137.8	133.7	129.5	125.4	121.3
	170.0	159.0	154.7	150.5	146.2	142.0	137.7	133.5	129.2	125.0
	175.0	163.6	159.3	154.9	150.5	146.1	141.8	137.4	133.0	128.6
	180.0	168.3	163.8	159.3	154.8	150.3	145.8	141.3	136.8	132.3
	185.0	173.0	168.4	163.7	159.1	154.5	149.9	145.2	140.6	136.0
	190.0	177.7	172.9	168.2	163.4	158.7	153.9	149.2	144.4	139.7
	195.0	182.3	177.5	172.6	167.7	162.8	158.0	153.1	148.2	143.3
	200.0	187.0	182.0	177.0	172.0	167.0	162.0	157.0	152.0	147.0
	205.0	191.7	186.6	181.4	176.3	171.2	166.1	160.9	155.8	150.7

(continued)

Table 2.2 *(continued)*

% of 1RM	100.0	93.5	91.0	88.5	86.0	83.5	81.0	78.5	76.0	73.5
Repetitions	1	2	3	4	5	6	7	8	9	10
Weight lifted	210.0	196.4	191.1	185.9	180.6	175.4	170.1	164.9	159.6	154.4
(lbs)	215.0	201.0	195.7	190.3	184.9	179.5	174.2	168.8	163.4	158.0
	220.0	205.7	200.2	194.7	189.2	183.7	178.2	182.7	167.2	161.7
	225.0	210.4	204.8	199.1	193.5	187.9	182.3	176.6	171.0	165.4
	230.0	215.1	209.3	203.6	197.8	192.1	186.3	180.6	174.8	169.1
	235.0	219.7	213.9	208.0	202.1	196.2	190.4	184.5	178.6	172.7
	240.0	224.4	218.4	212.4	206.4	200.4	194.4	188.4	182.4	176.4
	245.0	229.1	223.0	216.8	210.7	204.6	198.5	192.3	186.2	180.1
	250.0	233.8	227.5	221.3	215.0	208.8	202.5	196.3	190.0	183.8
	255.0	238.4	232.1	225.7	219.3	212.9	206.6	200.2	193.8	187.4
	260.0	243.1	236.6	230.1	223.6	217.1	210.6	204.1	197.6	191.2
	265.0	247.8	241.2	234.5	227.9	221.3	214.7	208.1	201.4	194.8
	270.0	252.5	245.7	239.0	232.2	225.5	218.7	212.0	205.2	198.5
	275.0	257.1	250.3	243.4	236.5	229.6	222.8	215.9	209.0	202.1
	280.0	261.8	254.8	247.8	240.8	233.8	226.8	219.8	212.8	205.8
	285.0	266.5	259.4	252.2	245.1	238.0	230.9	223.7	216.6	209.5
	290.0	271.2	263.9	256.7	249.4	242.5	234.9	227.7	220.4	213.2
	295.0	275.9	268.5	261.1	253.7	246.3	239.0	231.6	224.2	216.8
	300.0	280.5	273.0	265.5	258.0	250.5	243.0	235.5	228.0	220.5
	305.0	285.2	277.6	269.9	262.3	254.7	247.1	239.4	231.8	224.2
	310.0	289.9	282.1	274.4	266.6	258.9	251.1	243.4	235.6	227.9
	315.0	294.5	286.7	278.8	270.9	263.0	255.2	247.3	239.4	231.5
	320.0	299.2	291.2	283.2	275.2	267.2	259.2	251.2	243.2	235.2
	325.0	303.9	295.8	287.6	279.5	271.4	263.3	255.1	247.0	238.9
	330.0	308.6	300.3	292.1	283.8	275.9	267.3	259.1	250.8	242.6
	335.0	313.2	304.9	296.5	288.1	279.7	271.4	263.0	254.6	246.2
	340.0	317.9	309.4	300.9	292.4	283.9	275.4	266.9	258.4	249.9
	345.0	322.6	314.0	305.3	296.7	288.1	279.5	270.8	262.2	253.6
	350.0	327.3	318.5	309.8	301.0	292.3	283.6	274.8	266.0	257.3
	355.0	331.9	323.1	314.2	305.3	296.4	287.6	278.7	269.8	260.9
	360.0	336.6	327.6	318.6	309.6	300.6	291.6	282.6	273.6	264.6
	365.0	341.3	332.2	323.0	313.9	304.8	295.7	286.5	277.4	268.3
	370.0	346.0	336.7	327.5	318.2	309.0	299.7	290.5	281.2	272.0
	375.0	350.6	341.3	331.9	322.5	313.1	303.8	294.4	285.0	275.6
	380.0	355.3	345.8	336.3	326.8	317.3	307.8	298.3	288.8	279.3
	385.0	360.0	350.4	340.7	331.1	321.5	311.9	302.2	292.6	283.0
	390.0	364.7	354.9	345.2	335.4	325.7	315.9	306.2	296.4	286.7
	395.0	364.7	354.9	345.2	335.4	325.7	315.9	306.2	296.4	286.7
	400.0	374.0	364.0	354.0	344.0	334.0	324.0	314.0	304.0	294.0
	405.0	378.7	368.6	358.4	348.3	338.2	328.1	317.9	307.8	297.7
	410.0	383.4	373.1	362.9	352.6	342.4	332.1	321.9	311.6	301.4
	415.0	388.0	377.7	367.3	356.9	346.5	336.2	325.8	315.4	305.0

420.0	392.7	382.2	371.7	361.2	350.7	340.2	329.7	319.2	308.7
425.0	397.4	386.8	376.1	365.5	354.9	344.3	333.6	323.0	312.4
430.0	402.1	391.3	380.6	369.8	359.1	348.3	337.6	326.8	316.1
435.0	406.7	395.9	385.0	374.1	363.2	352.4	341.5	330.6	319.7
440.0	411.4	400.4	389.4	378.4	367.4	356.4	345.4	334.4	323.4
445.0	416.1	405.0	393.8	382.7	371.6	360.5	349.3	338.2	327.1
450.0	420.8	409.5	398.3	387.0	375.8	364.5	353.3	342.0	330.8
455.0	425.4	414.1	402.7	391.3	379.9	368.6	357.2	345.8	334.4

Reprinted, by permission, from *Stronger arms and upper body* by Sean Cochran and Tom House, copyright 2000, Human Kinetics, Champaign, IL.

For example, let's say you were able to perform 10 repetitions of a bench press using a 305-pound weight. Under the 10 repetitions column, find 305 pounds. Look left across that row to the first column (1 repetition). This weight, 415 pounds, would be your 1RM.

SQUAT JUMP

The squat jump is a plyometric drill that can be used to test muscular power in the lower body. (See chapter 7 for more on plyometric exercises.) All you need for this drill is a flat surface and an assistant with a stopwatch.

Procedure

1. Stand with your feet shoulder-width apart. Lock your fingers behind your head, elbows pointed out.

2. When the timer says, "Go" and starts the stopwatch, drop to a squat position and explosively jump as high as you can.

3. Land in the squat position and immediately jump again. Repeat for 10 seconds, performing as many squat jumps as you can.

POWER PUSH-UP

For the power push-up, you will need a medicine ball (five to eight pounds) or a similar object to push off from.

Procedure

1. Assume a push-up position with your hands on the ball, elbows straight.

2. When the timer says, "Go" and starts the stopwatch, remove your hands from the ball and drop to the ground. When your hands touch the ground, they should be a little more than shoulder-width apart. Flex your elbows and drop lower until your chest touches the medicine ball.

3. Immediately push up, fully extending your elbows. Return your hands to the medicine ball.

4. Repeat for 30 seconds, performing as many push-ups as you can.

TWO-MILE RUN

You can perform this test on a running track or on any marked two-mile course. A running track provides the best surface for accurate testing because it is a flat running surface and it is premeasured.

Procedure

1. Begin at the starting line.

2. When the timer says, "Go" and starts the stopwatch, begin running the course.

3. Complete the course as quickly as possible while maintaining a steady pace for the entire two miles. The timer can help you keep a steady pace by noting your quarter-mile times and comparing them.

4. When you cross the finish line, the timer stops the stopwatch and records your time.

THREE-MINUTE STEP TEST

For this test, you will need a 12-inch box to step on. Make sure the box is stable and has a flat, nonslip surface with good traction. It's a good idea to have two people help you with this test—one to keep track of time and one to count the number of steps you complete.

Procedure

1. Stand in front of the box with your feet shoulder-width apart, hands down by your sides.

2. When the timer says, "Go" and starts the stopwatch, step onto the box with one foot, bring the other foot up to meet it, then step down one foot at a time. You can rest your hands on your hips or move them as if you were running.

3. Perform as many steps as you can in three minutes. Be sure to pace yourself and use correct form.

LINE DRILL

You will need five cones to mark off the distances on the running track. Place one cone at the starting point and cones at 38 feet, 94 feet, 150 feet, and 188 feet from the starting cone. (You can also use a normally marked basketball court. On the basketball court, you will begin at the baseline and run to the near free-throw line, midcourt line, far free-throw line, and far baseline, touching the lines with your foot.)

Procedure

1. Begin at the starting cone (point A).

2. When the timer says, "Go" and starts the stopwatch, sprint from point A to the second cone (point B) and touch the cone with your foot. Return to point A.

3. Sprint from point A to the third cone (point C). Touch the cone with your foot. Return to point A.

4. Sprint from point A to the fourth cone (point D). Touch the cone with your foot. Return to point A.

5. Sprint from point A to the fifth cone (point E). Touch the cone with your foot. Return to point A.

6. The timer stops the stopwatch when you pass point A.

7. After a two-minute rest, repeat the test. Repeat the cycle three more times, with a two-minute rest between each time, and average the time of the four trials.

SHUTTLE RUN

You will need two cones. Set one cone at the starting line and one cone 25 yards from the starting cone.

Procedure

1. Begin at the starting cone (point A).

2. When the timer says, "Go" and begins the stopwatch, sprint to the cone 25 yards away (point B) and touch the cone with your foot. Return to point A.

3. Sprint between points A and B a total of six times for a total of 300 yards. Be sure to touch the cones with your foot each time.

4. The timer stops the stopwatch when you pass point A after the sixth trip.

5. Rest for five minutes, then perform the test again. Average the two times.

20-YARD DASH

Set up marked start and finish lines 20 yards apart on a running track or other flat running surface. You may want to allow an extra 20 yards past the finish line for deceleration.

Procedure

1. Set up behind the starting line with one or two hands touching the ground.

2. When the timer says, "Go" and starts the stopwatch, run to the finish line as fast as you can.

3. Rest for two minutes and return to the starting line.

4. Repeat the test, then average the results of the two trials.

T-TEST

You will need four cones to mark the course on a flat floor with good traction (a basketball court, for example). Set a cone at the starting point (point A). Set a cone 10 yards in a straight line from the starting cone (point B). Set cones 5 yards to the left of point B (point C) and 5 yards to the right of point B (point D). On the floor the setup should resemble a capital letter T.

Procedure

1. Begin at point A.

2. When the timer says, "Go" and starts the stopwatch, sprint from point A to point B. Touch the base of the cone at point B with your right hand.

3. Shuffle to the left to point C. When shuffling, face forward and do not cross your feet. Touch the base of the cone at point C with your left hand.

4. Shuffle to the right to point D. Touch the base of the cone at point D with your right hand.

5. Shuffle back to point B and touch the base of the cone at point B with your left hand.

6. Run backward from point B to point A. The timer stops the stopwatch when you cross point A. (You may want to have a safety mat set up behind point A in case you fall while running backward.)

7. Rest two minutes between trials. Repeat the test a second time and use the best time of the two trials.

EDGREN SIDE STEP TEST

You will need to mark the testing area with tape on a flat gymnasium floor. Place a straight piece of tape on the floor to mark the starting line. Place tape 3 feet to the right of the starting line and 3 feet to the left of the starting line. Place tape 6 feet to the right of the starting line and 6 feet to the left of the starting line. You now have a 12-foot section of floor divided into four 3-foot sections.

Procedure

1. Begin with your feet straddling the starting line (the middle line).

2. When the timer says, "Go" and starts the stopwatch, sidestep to the right until your right foot touches or crosses the outside line to the right.

3. Sidestep to the left until your left foot touches or crosses the outside line to the left.

4. Sidestep back and forth, right to left and left to right, as quickly as you can for 10 seconds.

5. You score a point each time you cross a 3-foot section of floor. (For example, from the starting line to the far right outside line would be worth two points: one for the 3-foot section from the starting line to the first dividing line, one for the section from the first dividing line to the outside line.) You lose a point if your feet cross or if you fail to touch or cross an outside line.

SIT-AND-REACH TEST

If you don't have access to a sit-and-reach box, you can use a measuring tape or yard stick instead. Place the yard stick on top of a 12-inch box or tape the measuring tape to the top of the box.

Procedure

1. Take off your shoes. Sit with your feet 12 inches apart, toes pointed up, heels flat against the side of the box.

2. Lean forward and touch the measuring slide on top of the sit-and-reach box with your fingertips. (Or touch the end of the yard stick or measuring tape.)

3. Slowly reach forward with both hands, moving the measuring tape or yard stick across the top of the box. Reach as far as possible and hold the farthest position momentarily. For the best stretch, exhale when reaching and drop your head between your arms.

4. The person helping you with your fitness tests can hold your knees down to keep them straight, if necessary.

5. Repeat three times and record the best score of the three trials.

SUMMARY

These first two chapters present a great deal of information. Chapter 1 included a brief introduction to different styles of martial arts and provided information on the physical requirements of many of the martial arts. This chapter introduces a series of testing procedures and protocols to help you develop your training program. After reading these first two chapters, you can see how necessary it is to implement a conditioning program into your martial arts training. A conditioning program along with classroom training is required to achieve optimal performance.

CHAPTER 3

FLEXIBILITY FOR PUNCHING, KICKING, AND SPARRING

Almost anyone who has been involved or even interested in martial arts has heard that you must be flexible to begin learning martial arts. This notion is entirely false. You'll recall from chapter 1 that some martial arts require more flexibility than others, but flexibility is not a requirement to become involved in martial arts. An improvement in your flexibility is a direct result of your martial arts training, and for optimal performance in certain styles, extensive flexibility training is required.

Flexibility is the range of motion (ROM) around a joint. Many martial arts require a wide range of motion within the joints for certain skills. For example, a turning heel kick in taekwondo requires a wide range of motion around the ball-and-socket joint of the hip and the hinge joint of the knee. You need a certain degree of flexibility to perform many of the techniques in martial arts. Flexibility work enhances your physical performance in three ways:

- It improves your ability to move through the full range of motion around a joint, which helps in developing muscular skill movements.
- It decreases the risk of injury.
- It develops efficiency in integrated neuromuscular movements.

Before we introduce specific flexibility exercises, let's review when and where to implement flexibility work in your training program.

WARM-UP

You should never do flexibility exercises without a proper warm-up. Why? When "cold," muscles and joints are at a greater risk of injury than if the body is warmed up before performing flexibility exercises. Here are the goals of a warm-up:

- To increase the core temperature of the body by a few degrees
- To increase blood flow to working muscles
- To improve neuromuscular firing
- To increase flow of oxygen through the muscular system

You can see that a warm-up is essential for preparing the body to work. A general warm-up should consist of a 5- to 10-minute period of low-intensity aerobic activity (for example, light jogging, stationary bicycling, or brisk walking).

You should perform flexibility exercises before and after resistance training, martial arts practice, or competition. This will help prevent injury, assist in the warm-up, and increase flexibility. After you exercise, your muscle temperatures are elevated. Because of this rise in temperature, you can make greater strides in developing flexibility.

TYPES OF FLEXIBILITY EXERCISES

Flexibility work can be separated into three different categories: active, passive, and static.

Active flexibility work occurs when the person performing the exercises supplies the force for the exercises. For example, during a sitting toe touch the person supplies the force by placing the hands over the toes.

Passive flexibility exercises usually require a partner or device that provides the force during the exercise. The majority of passive flexibility work is categorized as proprioceptive neuromuscular facilitation (PNF), which uses a partner to passively activate the muscle. For example, during a supine hamstring exercise, a push/pull movement is provided by a partner or device, such as a towel.

Static flexibility exercises consist of a constant flex held in one position for 10 to 30 seconds. A static flex includes a relaxation followed by a contraction. A groin flexibility exercise is an example of a static exercise in which the adductors of the leg are passively relaxed, then contracted.

FLEXIBILITY EXERCISES

Following is a list of 14 flexibility exercises that should be an integral part of your training program. Because of the wide variety of muscular actions required by martial arts, you should perform a series of flexibility exercises for the entire body. Certain people may require extra attention to certain joints in flexibility work. Use these exercises as a guide, adjusting them to your needs.

CALF STRETCH

Muscles trained: Soleus, gastrocnemius.

Preparation: Stand with your palms on the floor, knees slightly bent, and weight on the balls of your feet.

Action: Press your left heel to the ground. Hold for 20 seconds. Repeat with the right heel.

SEATED GROIN STRETCH

Muscles trained: Adductors of leg.

Preparation: Sit on the ground with your legs folded, feet together, and elbows placed on knees.

Action: Press your knees down toward the floor, assisting with pressure from elbows on knees. Hold for 20 seconds.

STRADDLE GROIN STRETCH

Muscles trained: Adductors of leg, hamstrings, calves.

Preparation: Sit on the floor with your legs straddled and backs of knees flat on the floor.

Action: Extend your left hand over the left foot. Press the foot out into the hand and bring chest down toward knee. Hold for 20 seconds. Repeat action on right leg.

THIGH LUNGE

Muscles trained: Hip flexors, quadriceps.

Preparation: Stand upright with your left leg forward and left knee flexed to a position directly above left ankle. Keep your left foot flat on the ground. Keep the right leg straight.

Action: Lower your torso until the left thigh is parallel to the floor. Maintain straight posture in upper body. Repeat action with the right leg.

SIDE QUAD FLEX

Muscles trained: Quadriceps, iliopsoas.

Preparation: Lie on your side with both legs extended straight.

Action: Bend your left knee. Pull the left leg toward buttocks with left hand. Hold for 20 seconds. Repeat action with the right leg.

SIDE LUNGE STRETCH

Muscles trained: Adductors, abductors.

Preparation: Place your feet in a wide stance with both feet facing forward. Place your hands on the floor in front of torso. Keep your heels on the ground.

Action: Lean your upper body toward left foot, bending left knee to a 90-degree angle, keeping the right leg straight. Hold position for 20 seconds. Repeat on the opposite side.

SINGLE-ARM SIDE BEND

Muscles trained: Obliques, latissimus dorsi, serratus anterior.

Preparation: Stand with your feet shoulder-width apart, torso upright, and both hands on hips.

Action: Bend the upper torso toward the right side. Extend your left arm over your head, keeping right hand on hip or held loosely at your waist. Keep the torso straight; do not bend the upper body forward or backward. Hold for 20 seconds. Repeat on the opposite side.

SUPERMANS (ALTERNATING ARMS)

Muscles trained: Psoas major, quadratus lumborum, spinalis group.

Preparation: Lie flat on floor, face down, arms extended over your head, and legs straight.

Action: Raise your left arm off the ground and right leg from hip. Keep the leg and arm straight. Hold for 20 seconds. Repeat by raising the right arm and left leg off the ground.

BACK FLEXION

Muscles trained: Erector spinae, interspinals.

Preparation: Place your hands and knees on floor. Keep your back straight and face the floor.

Action: Arch your back down toward floor, keeping the arms straight. Adjust your head to face forward. Hold for 20 seconds.

BACK EXTENSION

Muscles trained: Erector spinae, interspinals.

Preparation: Place your hands and knees on floor. Keep your back straight and face the floor.

Action: Arch back up, keeping arms straight. Hold for 20 seconds.

NECK LEFT TO RIGHT

Muscle trained: Sternocleidomastoid.

Preparation: Stand straight with your hands on your hips.

Action: Turn your head to the left. Hold for 20 seconds. Repeat to the right.

NECK SIDE TO SIDE

Muscles trained: Sternocleidomastoid, trapezius.

Preparation: Stand straight with your hands on your hips.

Action: Facing forward, bend your head toward the right. Hold for 20 seconds. Repeat to the left side.

ARM CROSS

Muscles trained: Latissimus dorsi, teres major.

Preparation: Stand upright with your feet shoulder-width apart.

Action: Cross your left arm over your chest at shoulder height. Grasp the left arm with the right hand. Hold for 20 seconds. Repeat with the opposite arm.

ARM FLEXION

Muscles trained: Triceps, latissimus dorsi.

Position: Stand upright with your feet shoulder-width apart.

Action: Reach your left hand behind your head toward right scapula. Grasp the left arm with the right hand. Hold position for 20 seconds. Repeat with the right arm and left hand.

SUMMARY

The flexibility exercises presented in this chapter provide a complete head-to-toe approach to flexibility. Remember to perform flexibility work for all areas of the body, and tailor your program specifically to your martial art. Implement flexibility work into your everyday martial arts training. The ideal times to perform flexibility exercises are before and after practice, resistance training, and competition.

CHAPTER 4

JOINT-STABILIZATION FOR PROPER TECHNIQUE

All martial arts techniques require

numerous neuromuscular actions. Many muscles are required to concentrically and eccentrically contract around your joints to perform certain movements. For example, when performing a side kick in taekwondo, you require your body to extend and retract your leg in the kick. Two different sets of muscles are asked to do these two separate actions in a fluid motion. Stress is placed on all sets of muscles involved in the kick to accelerate and decelerate your leg. The extension and retraction of the kick are opposite actions, but each requires the same amounts of force generated by opposing muscles to complete the kick. Every small and large muscle in the integrated neuromuscular pattern of this kick needs to have equal power, strength, endurance, and flexibility to generate force for efficiency and prevention of injury.

You are only as strong as your weakest link. If one muscle in the series of muscles that extends or retracts this kick is weak, your kick will be less than optimal, and you will increase the possibility of injury to this muscle if it cannot take the amount of force. Joint-stabilization exercises are preventive in nature and focus on balancing your muscular system.

THE WHYS OF JOINT STABILIZATION

Any muscular action in the body has a concentric action (shortening of the muscle) and an eccentric action (lengthening of the muscle) supported by surrounding muscles called synergists. All muscles in these three categories have integrated functions. They work together as a unit to perform neuromuscular movements. Let's take a closer look at these three categories of muscular actions.

An agonist is the muscle most directly involved in creating a concentric skeletal movement. Agonists are also referred to as prime movers. When you throw a side kick, the hip extensors and flexors of the knee are the agonists of the movement.

Antagonists are the muscles that slow down or stop the movement created by the agonists. They counter the contraction of agonists in the skeletal movement. In the side kick, the flexors of the hip and extensors of the knee are the antagonists of the movement.

Synergists are the muscles that assist or are indirectly involved in supporting the agonists and antagonists as they perform skeletal movement. They are also referred to as secondary movers. The adductors and abductors are synergists during a side kick.

You can see that agonists, antagonists, and synergists are required to maintain functioning throughout an entire action and during this time have large amounts of force placed on them. For optimal performance and reduced risk of injury to the muscular system, each muscle involved in a movement (agonist, antagonist, and synergist) must have balanced ratios of power, strength, and endurance. This balance in the system is termed hypertrophic parity.

THE IMPORTANCE OF JOINT-STABILIZATION EXERCISES

Often, training programs focus on isolated primary-mover-oriented strength training. As you know, neuromuscular actions in the body are integrated and require a balance in the system. In an isolated primary-mover-oriented training system, many of the synergist muscles (the small muscles) are ignored. The result is less-than-optimal performance and quite often injury to such muscles. Synergists often ignored in isolation-oriented training are the rotator cuff muscles (supraspinatus, infraspinatus, teres minor, and subscapularis). These four muscles are used as synergists in many shoulder and arm actions in which adduction, abduction, supination, or pronation of the upper arm takes place.

One objective of joint-stabilization exercises is to prevent these two situations—less-than-optimal performance and increased risk of injury—from occurring. Another reason to implement joint-stabilization exercises is to develop optimal levels of muscular strength and endurance in the synergists of your muscular system, otherwise known as hypertrophic parity. Hypertrophic parity can be defined as equilibrium in the muscular system's ratios of strength, endurance, and power.

OPEN- AND CLOSED-CHAIN TRAINING

You now have a clear understanding of the benefits, the importance, and the effects of joint-stabilization exercises. Let's take a look at the specific training procedures and exercises that are encompassed in joint-stabilization work. Joint-stabilization work is a combination of open-chain and closed-chain exercises, which function together to create hypertrophic parity (balance) within your muscular system.

Closed-chain training is any resistance exercises that happen when your feet are in contact with the ground. Your own body weight or weight added to your center of gravity is used for resistance purposes. An example of a closed-chain exercise is a push-up. The resistance comes from your own body weight as you lower yourself toward the ground.

Open-chain training is the use of outside sources of resistance for training. The feet are not in contact with the ground during open-chain training. Exercises are performed with the assistance of light dumbbells, elastic cords, or medicine balls. An example of an open-chain exercise is a dumbbell rotator cuff exercise. The dumbbell provides the resistance.

Both open- and closed-chain training are beneficial to developing the synergist muscles and can be used to develop strength, endurance, and power in the primary movers. When used together, open- and closed-chain exercises develop muscular balance in the body; this balance is called *hypertrophic parity*.

The majority of closed-chain joint-stabilization work is termed *bodywork*. Bodywork is using your own body weight as resistance through a series of exercises that focus on the development of strength and endurance of the synergist muscles. Research performed by Functional Fitness Paradigms has shown that bodywork is the safest and fastest resistance-training method for the development of hypertrophic parity.

Open-chain exercises focus on the development of endurance and strength within the synergists through all specified joint ranges of motion. Open-chain exercises coupled with closed-chain exercises provide a complete joint-stabilization program that reduces the risk of injury and leads to the development of hypertrophic parity.

The series that follows is the recommended series of closed- and open-chain exercises for your joint-stabilization program. You should perform closed-chain bodywork exercises first because they are of lower intensity. Then proceed to open-chain exercises. In the grand scheme of things, your joint-stabilization exercises should follow your flexibility work. You should do joint-stabilization exercises daily and incorporate them into your resistance-training program.

CLOSED-CHAIN EXERCISES

Each of the closed-chain exercises that follow should be done to your own level of tolerance. Perform each exercise in various positions (e.g., hand and shoulder rotations) to ensure that all ranges of motion of the synergists are trained accordingly. Multiple sets are not necessary because the combined volume of your closed-chain and open-chain exercises is sufficient in developing strength within these muscles. Repetitions can vary from one to five for each position of the exercise. You should determine your own repetition range based on your own tolerance.

Many of the following exercises refer to the flex-T position. Flex-T describes a position of optimal joint integrity for the shoulders and elbows when the elbows are at shoulder height slightly in front of the shoulder joints. This position will help protect your shoulders from injury.

Many of the fitness tests in this chapter are adapted, by permission, from *Stronger Arms and Upper Body* by Sean Cochran and Tom House, copyright 2000, Human Kinetics, Champaign, IL.

BUTT-UPS

Muscles trained: Shoulder capsule complex, rotator cuff.

Position: Sit on the floor with your back and legs straight. Keep your head and shoulders forward and the elbows bent.

Action: Hold your hands next to your hips, first facing forward then facing backward, inward, and outward. Lift your butt two to three inches from the floor. Perform three to five repetitions for each hand position.

FLEX-T PUSH-UPS

Muscles trained: Shoulder capsule complex, rotator cuff, abdominals and low back structure, triceps, pectoralis.

Position: Assume a basic push-up position with your elbows at shoulder height in a flex-T and palms on the floor.

Action: Perform three to five push-ups with your hands in a neutral position, fingertips facing forward. Then perform three to five push-ups with your fingertips turned toward you. Finally, perform three to five push-ups with your fingertips facing away from you.

ONE-ARM SIDE-UPS

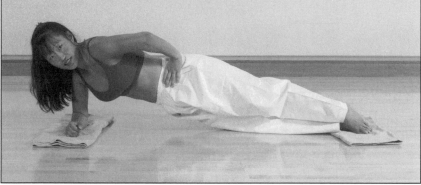

Muscles trained: Abdominals, low back structure, obliques, shoulder capsule complex.

Position: Lie on your side with your lower forearm on the ground and the elbow directly beneath your shoulder. You may use small mats or folded towels under your elbow and feet for comfort. Place your upper hand on your hip.

Action: Raise your body using your torso muscles. Perform three to nine repetitions of up-and-down movement. Then while in the up position, rotate hips half a turn and repeat hip rotation for three to nine repetitions. Repeat on the opposite side.

ONE-ARM PUSH-UPS

Muscles trained: Shoulder capsule complex, rhomboids.

Position: Lie on your side with the lower forearm on the ground and the elbow directly beneath your shoulder. Place your upper hand on the ground in a plum line from your upper shoulder.

Action: Lean into your upper hand and press your body up using an extension of the arm. This will work the arm and shoulder muscles. Perform three to five repetitions.

OPEN-CHAIN EXERCISES

After proceeding through the closed-chain joint-stabilization exercises, move on to the open-chain exercises. The focus again is on the development of your synergists through all ranges of motion. Very little equipment is needed. You should have a medicine ball, light dumbbells (three to five pounds), and an elastic cord.

Perform these exercises to your own level of tolerance. Do two to five repetitions per exercise per angle. Remember: one set of each exercise is plenty. These open-chain exercises complement the closed-chain (bodywork) exercises. You should use the sets of protocols together for a complete joint-stabilization program.

Light Dumbbell Exercises

Remember to use light weights, maintain proper body position, and follow the correct movement pattern of the exercise.

DUMBBELL CROSSES

Muscles trained: Rotator cuff, shoulder capsule complex.

Position: Hold the dumbbells in your hands. Stand straight with your arms at sides and your feet shoulder-width apart.

Action: Raise your left arm straight across your body to the right shoulder with the palm down. Lower the dumbbell to side. Repeat with right arm. Perform three to five repetitions. Repeat movement with palms facing in and palms facing out.

FLEX-T ROTATORS

Muscles trained: Rotator cuff, rhomboids, shoulder capsule complex, scapular stabilizers.

Position: Stand straight with your feet shoulder-width apart. Raise your elbows to shoulder level and bend 90 degrees, slightly in front of shoulder capsules.

Action: With your palms facing forward, rotate your forearms to a position parallel to the floor, dumbbells on the same plane as your shoulders. Return to the starting position. Repeat with your palms facing in and out. Perform three to five repetitions in each position.

UPRIGHT FLYS

Muscles trained: Shoulder capsule complex rotator cuff.

Position: Stand with your head in front of your navel, feet shoulder-width apart, knees bent. Hold the dumbbells with your arms in front of your pelvis, palms facing in. Always keep your elbows in front of your shoulder capsules.

Action: Raise the dumbbells together in an upright motion to shoulder level. Extend the arms straight out to the sides. Lower the dumbbells to the starting position keeping your palms facing in. Raise the dumbbells again to shoulder level then out to your sides, rotating the palms back. Lower the dumbbells to starting position. Finally, raise the dumbbells again to shoulder level, then out to your sides, rotating the palms forward as you extend your arms. Lower the dumbbells to starting position. Perform three to five repetitions with each position and movement.

BUTTERFLIES

Muscles trained: Shoulder capsule complex and deltoids.

Preparation: Stand straight with your feet shoulder-width apart. Hold the dumbbells together, palms facing each other, in front of your pelvis.

Action: Raise the dumbbells in a circular action above forehead. Return to starting position. Perform three to nine repetitions.

BENT-OVER PULLS

Muscles trained: Shoulder capsule complex, scapular stabilizers.

Preparation: Stand with your feet slightly wider than shoulder width and your hips placed in position between legs. Keep your back flat. Dumbbells are on floor, vertically aligned with shoulders.

Action: Alternate raising the right and left dumbbells off the floor, palms facing you. Maintain an elbow position vertically aligned with shoulder. Repeat the exercise with palms facing in and facing out. Perform three to five repetitions at each angle.

BENT-OVER FLYS

Muscles trained: Shoulder capsule complex, rhomboids, scapular stabilizers.

Preparation: Keep your feet slightly wider than shoulder width and hips placed in position between legs. Keep the back flat. Dumbbells are on floor together in front of torso.

Action: Raise the dumbbells together to chest level. Extend your arms straight out. Return to the starting position. Perform three to nine repetitions.

Elastic Cord Exercises

Before beginning the elastic cord exercises, make sure the cords are completely secured and are at the correct tension. Maintain correct body position and movement pattern during the exercises.

SHOULDER CIRCLES

Muscles trained: Shoulder capsule complex.

Preparation: Stand with your feet shoulder-width apart, knees bent, torso slightly forward, elbows at shoulder height bent at a 90-degree angle.

Action: Maintain a 90-degree bend in the elbow. Circle shoulder capsule forward three to nine repetitions. Reverse circle three to nine repetitions.

HITCHHIKERS

Muscles trained: Shoulder capsule complex, rotator cuff, elbow extensors.

Preparation: Stand with your feet shoulder-width apart, knees slightly bent, torso slightly forward. Place your right hand in front of forehead, right thumb pointing down.

Action: Extend right arm at elbow to straight position. Point right thumb up during movement. Return to starting position. Perform three to nine repetitions. Repeat with the left arm.

TRICEPS EXTENSIONS

Muscles trained: Triceps, shoulder capsule, rotator cuff, arm extensors.

Preparation: Stand with your feet shoulder-width apart, knees slightly bent, torso slightly forward. Place your right hand in front of left shoulder with right thumb pointing up.

Action: Extend your forearm back and down while rotating right thumb down. Return to start position. Perform three to nine repetitions. Repeat with the left arm.

INTERNAL ROTATION

Muscle trained: Rotator cuff.

Preparation: Stand with your feet shoulder-width apart, knees slightly bent, left elbow bent at 90 degrees and placed next to rib cage with elastic cord tensed. Hold the ends of the elastic cord in your hands.

Action: Pull your left forearm across to right side of body while keeping your left elbow at your rib cage. Return to the starting position. Perform three to nine repetitions. Repeat with the right arm.

EXTERNAL ROTATION

Muscle trained: Rotator cuff.

Preparation: Stand with your feet shoulder-width apart, knees slightly bent, right elbow bent at 90 degrees and placed next to rib cage, right hand on left side of body with elastic cord tensed. Hold the ends of the elastic cord in your hands.

Action: Pull your right hand to position horizontally in line with right elbow on rib cage. Return to start position. Perform three to nine repetitions. Repeat with the left arm.

REVERSE ROTATORS

Muscles trained: Shoulder capsule complex, rotator cuff.

Preparation: Stand with your feet shoulder-width apart, knees slightly bent, torso slightly forward, elbows bent at 90-degree angle, hands at shoulder level, palms facing down.

Action: Maintain a 90-degree bend in elbow. Lift forearms so palms face forward, keeping elbows at shoulder level. Return to the starting position. Perform three to nine repetitions.

Medicine Ball Exercises

During the medicine ball exercises, maintain correct body position and exercise movement pattern.

WIDE ELBOW MEDICINE BALL WALL TOSS

Muscles trained: Shoulder capsule, rotator cuff, arm extensors and flexors.

Preparation: Stand with your knees bent, elbows resting on wall six inches away from ears on each side of head, medicine ball in hands behind head.

Action: Throw the medicine ball against the wall, keeping elbows in contact with the wall. Return to the starting position with hands behind the head. Perform 45 to 60 throws.

Variation:

Narrow Elbow Medicine Ball Wall Toss: Stand with your knees bent, elbows resting on wall *next to ears,* medicine ball in hands behind head. Throw the medicine ball against the wall, keeping elbows in contact with the wall. Return to the starting position with hands behind head. Perform 45 to 60 throws.

RIGHT- AND LEFT-ARM WALL TOSS

Muscles trained: Shoulder capsule, rotator cuff, arm extensors and flexors.

Preparation: Stand 8 to 12 inches from a wall with your feet shoulder-width apart, knees bent, medicine ball in hand. Hold your tossing elbow at shoulder level.

Action: Throw and hold the medicine ball against the wall, keeping your elbow at shoulder level. Arm extension occurs at the elbow. Switch arms and repeat on the other side. Perform 45 to 60 tosses.

SUMMARY

Implementing joint-stabilization work in your training program will reduce the risk of injury within your synergist muscles and will develop muscular balance throughout your system. Remember to perform joint-stabilization work after flexibility exercises. A single set per exercise is ideal. Perform all exercises to your own level of tolerance.

CHAPTER 5

STRENGTHENING THE TORSO POWER ZONE

Much can be said about the role of the torso in martial arts. Composed of the muscular and skeletal structure of the abdomen and low back, the torso area affects a number of physical actions performed in the martial arts. The most important and basic functions of this region are flexion, extension, and rotation. The torso is also responsible for maintaining postural stability during movement. This chapter will review information on the functioning of the torso and provide you with exercises to strengthen the torso region.

Although the torso comprises the low back and abdomen, fitness books often place these two areas into separate categories for exercise purposes. The truth is that the abdomen and low back function together for movement and balance. Think of them as a unit. Any movement—be it flexion, extension, or rotation of the trunk—requires both muscle groups to function.

The muscles of the low back include the iliopsoas, psoas major, psoas minor, iliacus, quadratus lumborum, erector spinae, transverseospinals, and intertransversari. As you can see, quite a few muscles make up the low back. All of these are very important for the functioning of the torso.

On the front of the body, the torso consists of the abdominal muscles. These are the transversus abdominis, rectus abdominis, internal obliques, and external obliques. These muscles work in conjunction with the muscles of the low back to function as the torso. Before moving onto specific exercises for the region, let's take a moment to understand the functioning of this area.

THE TORSO IN MARTIAL ARTS

Many movements require flexion, extension, and rotation of the torso area. For example, when you perform a takedown in judo, all three of these actions are necessary to flip your opponent to the ground. When you perform a roundhouse kick in taekwondo, rotation and extension of the torso are necessary. The torso is also important in rotational torque.

Posture stabilization means maintaining a specific posture or body position during movement. When you perform movements in the martial arts, you are required to maintain a certain posture or body position. For example, when you're performing a side kick you need to rotate and extend the upper body backward. Throughout the action of the kick, you must hold (maintain) this body position. Postural stabilization requires strength and balance within the torso region, front to back. If balance and strength do not exist within the torso, then it will be quite difficult to perform martial art techniques optimally. It is important to spend time and effort on strengthening this region for success in the martial arts.

Another important area to cover in the discussion of the torso is rotational torque. Rotational torque is the amount of force produced through the rotation of a joint. The speed at which this force can be produced (also known as angular velocity) also is very important in the martial arts. Angular velocity is an object's rotational speed. Finally, the production of force and the velocity at which it is produced determines the amount of force produced.

What does this all mean? Well, let's take a closer look. Many movements in the martial arts require rotation of the hips and torso—for example, a roundhouse kick. A very rapid rotation of the hips and torso needs to occur to perform a roundhouse kick correctly. The quicker this occurs (rotation of the hip and torso), the faster (velocity) and more powerful (force produced and velocity) the kick.

The development of power is a direct result of the speed and amount of force that is produced. Obviously, a more powerful, faster kick is more effective. If you lack the ability to produce rotational force at a fast rate, your kicks and other techniques will be less effective. A torso that has a balance of strength in the abdomen and low back will result in

- enhanced ability to perform the necessary actions of flexion, extension, and rotation;
- maintenance of postural stabilization during martial art movements; and
- more rapid production of rotational force.

You should perform torso exercises a minimum of three days per week and a maximum of six days per week. After performing a proper warm-up, flexibility work, and joint-stabilization exercises, you will find it is an ideal point to implement torso exercises. It is not necessary to perform these exercises before every practice session, but it is highly recommended that you perform these exercises within your resistance-training program. Between one and three sets per exercise is recommended, and anywhere from 5 to 20 repetitions is ideal. As with all joint-stabilization exercises, customize your torso exercises to your own tolerance. Keep these thoughts in mind and your torso training will be a key to your success in the martial arts.

TORSO-STABILIZATION EXERCISES

Little equipment is needed for the torso-stabilization exercises. You may want a medicine ball and Physio ball, but a fundamentally sound program can be implemented without any equipment. These exercises are not separated into abdominal and low back sections. You should perform exercises for the abdomen and low back as a unit. If you find a slight variance in strength between your low back and abdomen, maintain a program that continues to train both your front and back sides. If you find an extreme difference in strength between your low back and abdomen, then it may be necessary to add additional exercises to work the weak area until muscular balance is developed.

LOW BACK PRESS

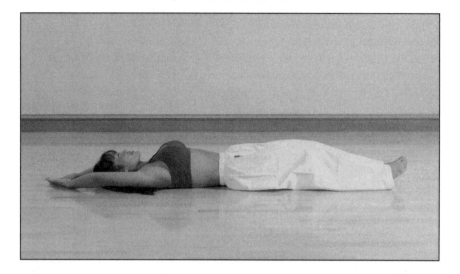

Muscles trained: Low back musculature structure, abdominal structure.

Preparation: Lie on the floor with your arms extended over your head, legs straight, and feet together.

Action: Press your back isometrically into the floor. Contract your abdomen and low back together. Hold press position for 15 to 20 seconds.

SINGLE-LEG LOW BACK RAISE

Muscles trained: Low back musculature structure, gluteals, hamstrings.

Preparation: Lie on the floor with your arms straight out to the sides or bent at the elbows. Bend the left knee with left foot flat on floor. Keep the right leg straight and raised off the ground, parallel to the upper portion of the left leg.

Action: Press your low back off the floor. Keep shoulders in contact with ground and low back parallel to position of right leg. Hold position for 15 to 20 seconds.

SUPERMANS (BOTH ARMS)

Muscles trained: Psoas major, quadratus lumborum, spinalis group.

Preparation: Lie face down on the floor with your arms extended and legs straight.

Action: Raise both of your arms off the ground and both legs from the hips. Keep the legs and arms straight. Hold for 20 seconds.

BALANCED BACK EXTENSION

Muscles trained: Erector spinae, interspinals.

Preparation: Place your hands and knees on the floor. Keep your back straight and look down at the floor.

Action: Raise your left arm and right leg off the ground. Reach your left arm straight out in front of you, and reach your right leg straight behind you. Keep your back straight. Hold for 10 seconds. Lower left arm and right leg. Repeat with right arm and left leg. Perform 3 to 15 repetitions and repeat.

ABDOMINAL CRUNCHES

Muscles trained: Transversus abdominis, rectus abdominis, internal obliques, external obliques.

Preparation: Lie flat on your back with your feet off the floor and knees bent at 90 degrees. Place your hands at the sides of your head.

Action: Raise shoulders and upper torso off the floor. Low back remains flat on the floor. Your head and neck remain in neutral position. Return to the starting position. Perform 15 to 25 repetitions.

ABDOMINAL SIDE CRUNCHES

Muscles trained: Transversus abdominis, rectus abdominis, internal oblique, external oblique.

Preparation: Lie flat on your back with your feet off the floor and knees bent at 90 degrees. Place hands at the sides of your head.

Action: Raise your shoulders and upper torso off the ground while rotating the right elbow toward your left knee. Return to the starting position. Repeat, bringing your left elbow toward your right knee. Perform 15 to 25 repetitions.

MEDICINE BALL ABDOMINAL CRUNCHES

Muscles trained: Transversus abdominis, rectus abdominis, internal obliques, external obliques.

Preparation: Lie flat on your back with your legs extended straight up, arms extended perpendicular to the floor, and medicine ball in your hands.

Action: Raise your shoulders and upper torso off the ground, lifting medicine ball toward feet. Head and neck remain in neutral position. Return to starting position. Perform 15 to 25 repetitions.

PHYSIO BALL LOW BACK EXTENSIONS

Muscles trained: Low back and abdominal structure, gluteals.

Preparation: Lie flat on your back with your arms extended to the sides and your feet placed on top of Physio ball.

Action: Press your butt and low back off the floor, keeping feet on the Physio ball. Hold the position for 15 to 30 seconds. Perform 3 to 20 repetitions.

PHYSIO BALL CRUNCHES

Muscles trained: Abdominal and low back structure.

Preparation: Place your low back on top of Physio ball with your feet set firmly on the floor, hands next to the sides of your head, and low back arched over top of Physio ball.

Action: While keeping your feet on the floor, raise shoulders and upper torso off the top of the Physio ball. Return to the starting position. Keep your head and neck in neutral position. Perform 15 to 25 repetitions.

PHYSIO BALL ROTATIONS

Muscles trained: Abdominal and low back structure.

Preparation: Place your shoulders and upper back on top of Physio ball. Firmly plant your feet on the floor. Keep your arms straight and perpendicular to the ground. Clasp hands in front of face.

Action: While maintaining body position, rotate your upper torso to the left, allowing head to rotate, too. Return to starting position. Repeat to the right side. Perform 15 to 25 repetitions.

PHYSIO BALL JACK KNIFE

Muscles trained: Abdominal structure, low back structure, hip flexors and extensors.

Preparation: Get into push-up position with feet on top of Physio ball. Maintain a straight low back and leg position. Face the floor.

Action: Maintaining push-up position, pull your knees into your chest while keeping back flat. Return to starting position. Perform 15 to 25 repetitions.

SUMMARY

Choose torso exercises that train the entire torso region: front (abdomen), back (low back), and sides (obliques). The ideal torso program is a single set of all exercises performed to your own tolerance with anywhere from 2 to 15 repetitions per exercise.

CHAPTER 6

CORE EXERCISES FOR PERFORMANCE IMPROVEMENT

The exercises presented up to this

point have focused on total body development. The martial arts incorporate the muscles of the entire body. For example, a side kick requires specific positions and movements to execute the kick. All these movements require use of the entire body.

To develop the body, you will find that integrative (total body) exercises need to be complemented with exercises that focus on a certain muscle or muscle groups. This is especially true if you find that a specific muscle or area of the body lacks in a certain category (muscular endurance, strength, or power) or has been injured in the past. Even though the martial arts require total body involvement, isolation exercises are recommended when pursuing the goals of greater strength, power, or muscular endurance.

Flexibility, joint-stabilization, and torso-stabilization exercises will "balance" your body when it comes to the endurance and strength factors of your small to large muscles. "Core" exercises focus on developing greater gains in strength, power, and endurance from total-body exercises down to isolation exercises. This gets you to the point of multijoint and single-joint exercises. The core exercises you will find in the next few chapters can be classified into either of these categories.

MULTIJOINT AND SINGLE-JOINT EXERCISES

Multijoint exercises are core exercises based on skeletal joint movements. A multijoint exercise involves moving more than one joint through a specified range of motion. A multijoint core exercise that appears in the next chapter is the power clean. A power clean requires the use of the entire body for flexion and extension of the ankles, knees, and hips.

An exercise is classified as a single-joint exercise when only one skeletal joint is moved through a range of motion during the action. A barbell curl is an example of a single-joint exercise, because the bar is lifted through a range of motion involving only the elbow joint.

When you are developing your resistance-training program for the martial arts, it is important to order your core exercises correctly. Perform multijoint exercises before single-joint exercises. Why? Well, think about the martial arts and what you know about their physical requirements. You know that the martial arts require integrative movements. Therefore in your training, you should perform integrative exercises for the purpose of cross-specificity. So it makes sense to do multijoint exercises before single-joint exercises since you use your whole body to perform martial arts movements; your training pattern should be similar. Some advanced techniques or the rehabilitation of an injury may dictate doing the opposite (single-joint before multijoint), but overall keep this rule as a general focus point.

> Place core multijoint exercises at the beginning of your program, and institute single-joint exercises second.

TRAIN "LARGE TO SMALL"

Another important factor is the "train large to small" sequence of exercises. This idea sequences your larger muscle group exercises first, then progresses toward smaller muscle groups. Always train synergists (joint-stabilization protocols) first for muscular balance. If you perform exercises for the larger muscle groups first, many of the smaller muscles will function to assist the primary movers. For example, during the squat (a multijoint exercise), the muscles of the entire lower body are used. If you were to perform leg extensions (a single-joint exercise) before squats, the benefits from the squat would be negated somewhat because you have already fatigued a muscle group used in the exercise.

PROGRESSION OF CORE EXERCISES

Perform a proper warm-up, flexibility exercises, torso-stabilization exercises, and joint-stabilization exercises before core exercises. Core exercises are not done daily because of the extensive muscular fatigue that occurs. A certain amount of recovery time (48 to 72 hours) is required for the muscles to restore themselves. Take a quick glance at chapter 1 for the parameters of muscle recovery.

Core exercises should be done on resistance-training days only. For optimal recovery a good rule of thumb is to separate core exercise days by a minimum of 48 hours. Chapter 10 provides further information on setting up your complete training program. You will also find examples of how to implement core exercises into a complete training program.

GUIDELINES

The following guidelines will help you develop core exercise protocols. Take a minute to review them.

• *Perform multijoint exercises first.* The martial arts contain integrated, total-body actions. For the purpose of specificity, place multijoint exercises first in your exercise order. Then move on to single-joint exercises.

• *Train large to small.* Train your larger muscle groups before exercising small muscles and synergists. Your secondary muscles and synergists act as stabilizers and may become fatigued if trained before your primary movers.

• *Include exercises in all three movement planes.* The martial arts require numerous muscular actions in various joint angles. For the purpose of specificity and muscular balance, incorporate exercises in all three movement planes (left to right, top to bottom, and front to back).

• *Train your muscles for specific outcomes in muscular endurance, strength, and power.* Use the training variables—load, intensity, volume, duration, and frequency—for a specific result in muscular endurance, strength, or power required by your martial art.

CORE EXERCISES

The following exercises provide a good foundation for the development of your core exercise program. You will need equipment for most of the exercises. Table 6.1 lists the exercises and required equipment. You should have a spotter help you when you perform any resistance training. Follow the exercise descriptions and use a weight you can lift correctly. Maintain the correct body position and movement pattern throughout the exercise.

Table 6.1   Equipment Needed for Core Exercises

Multijoint exercises	Equipment needed
Power clean	Barbell
Push press	Barbell
Squat	Barbell
Dumbbell bench press	Dumbbells, weight bench
Deadlift	Barbell
Lunges	Dumbbells
Bent-over barbell row	Barbell
Hang snatch	Barbell

Single-joint exercises	Equipment needed
Lat pulldown	Lat pulldown machine with overhead bar
Biceps barbell curl	Barbell
Reverse biceps barbell curl	Barbell
Triceps cable extension	Cable weight machine with overhead bar
Wide grip chin	Chin-up bar
Physio ball triceps push-up	Physio ball
Leg extension	Leg extension machine
Leg curl	Leg curl machine
Standing calf raise	Calf raise machine
Medicine ball skater	Medicine ball

POWER CLEAN

Muscles trained: Total body.

Preparation: Stand with your feet shoulder-width apart and flat on floor. Grab the bar in an overhand grip with your hands shoulder-width apart and arms extended straight. Bend your knees, positioning your hips below knee level. Keep your back flat and straight and hold your head and neck in a neutral position.

Action

First pull: Extend your legs, driving upward with your hips, keeping your back flat. With control, pull the bar off the floor to a position slightly below your knees. The bar remains close to your legs.

Second pull: Drive your hips forcefully up and forward. Your arms remain straight, your back stays flat, and the bar stays close to your thighs.

Third pull: Shrug your shoulders up, forcefully pulling the bar up. Keep the bar close to your torso. Extend onto the balls of your feet and continue to force your hips up explosively.

Finish position: Get the bar to the top of your shoulders by pulling yourself under the bar and catching it. Absorb the catch by bending your knees and lowering your hips. Rotate your elbows up to a position horizontally in line with your shoulders. Keep your back straight and extend your knees to end in an upright and straight body position.

PUSH PRESS

Muscles trained: Shoulder complex, arm extensors, hip extensors, low back, abdominal structure, upper back complex.

Preparation: Rest the bar on your shoulders with your elbows even with your shoulders, back straight, and your knees slightly bent.

Action: Explosively extend your arms up to a straight position. Bend your knees slightly and split your legs into a lunge position. Your back remains straight. Keep your head and neck in a neutral position.

SQUAT

Muscles trained: Quadriceps, hamstrings, hip flexors, hip extensors, low back, abdominal structure, gluteals.

Preparation: With your feet shoulder-width apart or slightly wider, place the bar on the back side of your shoulders. Grasp the bar with your hands shoulder-width apart, back straight, and head and neck in neutral position.

Action: Lower your hips by bending your knees, keeping your back straight. Bend your knees to a 90-degree position. From squat position, press the bar up by straightening your legs and elevating your hips up and forward.

DUMBBELL BENCH PRESS

Muscles trained: Pectoralis major, deltoids, triceps.

Preparation: Lie flat on a weight bench with your feet flat on the ground. Grasp the dumbbells at shoulder-width position.

Action: Extend your arms and press the dumbbells up. Maintain a flat back on the bench. Return to the starting position.

DEADLIFT

Muscles trained: Low back, hamstrings, gluteals.

Preparation: Stand with your feet shoulder-width apart or slightly wider. Grasp the bar with your hands at shoulder width. Your back is flat, hips lowered below knees, feet flat on floor, and head and neck in neutral position.

Action: While maintaining a flat back, drive your hips up and forward in a controlled manner, extending the knees to a straight position. Your back remains straight, head facing forward. Return to the starting position in a controlled manner.

LUNGES

Muscles trained: Quadriceps, gluteals, hamstrings.

Preparation: Stand with your back straight, head and neck in neutral position, and dumbbells at your sides. Place your left foot forward and your right foot behind your torso, leg straightened. Lift your right heel off the ground, but keep your left foot flat on the floor.

Action: Lower your hips straight down, keeping your torso upright, head facing forward. Bend your left knee to 90 degrees. Allow your back leg to bend at the knee to a comfortable position. Return to the starting position. Repeat and switch legs.

BENT-OVER BARBELL ROW

Muscles trained: Latissimus dorsi, rhomboids, scapular stabilizers, rear deltoids, low back, biceps.

Preparation: Stand with your feet shoulder-width apart, feet flat on floor, knees slightly bent, torso leaning forward slightly, back flat, head facing forward, and your arms straight. Grasp the barbell with your hands at shoulder width.

Action: While maintaining your body position, pull the bar up to mid-chest, squeezing your shoulder blades together. Return to the starting position and repeat.

HANG SNATCH

Muscles trained: Hip extensors, gluteals, knees extensors, low back, shoulder complex, triceps.

Preparation: Stand with your feet shoulder-width apart and flat on the floor, knees bent, back flat, and the bar at thigh level. Grasp the bar three to four inches wider than shoulder width, head facing forward.

Action: Lower the bar to a position slightly above your knees by lowering your hips. Extend your hips up and forward explosively, extending the knees to a straight position. Pull the bar up forcefully, bending the arms slightly. Elevate onto the balls of your feet. Pull yourself down and under the bar, extend the arms to a straight position, and catch the bar overhead. After catching the bar, straighten your knees and stand straight.

LAT PULLDOWN

Muscles trained: Latissimus dorsi, rhomboids, scapular stabilizers.

Preparation: Sit in the lat pulldown machine with your feet on the floor. Grasp the bar slightly wider than shoulder width. Keep your back straight, torso leaning slightly back, and your head and neck in neutral position.

Action: While maintaining upper-body posture, pull the bar down to your upper chest. Squeeze your shoulder blades together. Return to the starting position.

BICEPS BARBELL CURL

Muscles trained: Biceps.

Preparation: Stand with your feet shoulder-width apart and knees slightly bent. Grip the bar at shoulder width, palms facing up, bar resting at mid-thigh level, and your elbows next to rib cage.

Action: Curl the bar to shoulder height, maintaining elbow position. Return to the starting position and repeat.

REVERSE BICEPS BARBELL CURL

Muscles trained: Biceps brachii, forearms.

Preparation: Stand with your feet shoulder-width apart and your knees slightly bent. Grip the bar at shoulder width, palms facing down, bar resting at mid-thigh level, elbows next to rib cage.

Action: Curl the bar to shoulder height while maintaining upright torso position. Keep your elbows next to the rib cage. Return to the starting position and repeat.

TRICEPS CABLE EXTENSION

Muscles trained: Triceps.

Preparation: Stand with your feet shoulder-width apart, knees slightly bent, and torso upright. Grasp an overhead cable machine bar with your palms down at shoulder height and your elbows next to your rib cage.

Action: Press down on the bar, extending arms to straight position, keeping the elbows at your sides. Return to the starting position and repeat.

WIDE GRIP CHIN

Muscles trained: Latissimus dorsi, scapula stabilizers, rhomboids.

Preparation: Grasp the bar with your hands at elbow width. Your body remains in a stable position with the arms extended.

Action: Pull your body up to the bar, elevating your head above the bar and upper chest parallel to bar. Return to the starting position and repeat.

PHYSIO BALL TRICEPS PUSH-UP

Muscles trained: Triceps, pectoralis major, deltoids.

Preparation: Assume a push-up position on a Physio ball, with your legs and torso straight, back flat, arms extended straight, and head facing down. The Physio ball should be positioned underneath your chest.

Action: Bend your arms, lowering your chest to one inch from the Physio ball. Maintain a straight body position. Extend your arms to straight position. Repeat.

LEG EXTENSION

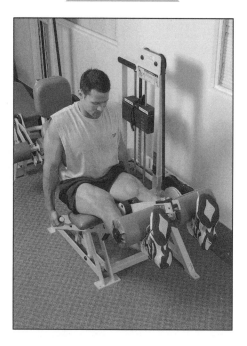

Muscles trained: Quadriceps.

Preparation: Sit in a leg extension machine with your torso slightly bent forward, pad resting on shins, and toes pointed up.

Action: Extend your legs to a straight position. Keep your toes pointing up. Return to the starting position and repeat.

LEG CURL

Muscles trained: Hamstrings.

Preparation: Lie face down on a leg curl machine with the pad resting on the back of your calves and toes pointing down.

Action: Curl your legs back toward your butt. Return to the starting position and repeat.

STANDING CALF RAISE

Muscles trained: Gastrocnemius, soleus.

Preparation: Place the balls of your feet on calf raise platform. Keep your knees slightly bent and calf machine pads resting on shoulders. Keep your torso straight and head facing forward.

Action: Straighten your knees while raising weight stack. Lower your heels toward the floor, then raise heels. Return heels to down position. Repeat.

MEDICINE BALL SKATER

Muscles trained: Adductors, abductors, gluteals.

Preparation: Stand with your feet four to six inches wider than shoulder width and feet pointed forward. Extend your arms forward horizontally in line with shoulders. Keep your torso straight and your hips lowered to a position between knees. Grasp a medicine ball in both hands.

Action: Shift your hips to the left, bending the left knee and extending the right leg. Shift your hips to the right, bending the right knee and extending the left leg. Repeat.

SUMMARY

The exercises in this chapter provide an excellent foundation for developing your core exercise program. Remember to be specific in both the physical requirements (strength and endurance) and biomechanical requirements (movement patterns) of your martial art. Allow proper recovery between core exercise training sessions, and slot your core exercises after your flexibility, torso, and joint-stabilization exercises. Keep these basic guidelines in mind when you are developing your core exercise program, and success will be within your reach.

CHAPTER 7

PLYOMETRICS FOR EXPLOSIVE MOVEMENTS

Plyometrics are exercises that focus

on developing the explosive action of muscles. Often plyometric exercises involve jumping, and many exercises require equipment such as a plyometric box, cone, or medicine ball. Plyometrics are often a part of athletes' training programs. You will find plyometric training fundamental to many sports such as football, basketball, ice hockey, and tennis. Notice that all these sports require powerful, quick, explosive movements. The majority of martial arts also require powerful, quick, explosive movements. Let's take a look at an example.

A side kick in taekwondo requires a person to extend and retract the entire lower leg in a horizontal plane. The optimal side kick, mechanically and physically, is quick, powerful, and explosive. From this example you can see a parallel between the explosive movements in the martial arts and the movements in the other sports mentioned. The conclusion is that plyometric training is as useful in physically developing the martial artist as it is for athletes in other sports.

PLYOMETRIC PROGRAM DESIGN

Before getting into program design, let me remind you that as with any other program in this book, a proper warm-up and flexibility session is required. Plyometrics place a lot of stress on the muscular system. Neglecting to perform a proper warm-up before plyometrics dramatically increases the risk of injury. As with the other resistance-training exercises, plyometrics follow a similar set of variables: intensity, volume, frequency, and recovery.

Remember that intensity refers to a percentage of maximal effort executed during a specific task. In relation to resistance training, intensity is the percentage of your 1-repetition maximum (1RM) for a certain exercise. Plyometrics involve the intensity variable, but it is measured differently. Intensity in plyometrics refers to the complexity of the exercise performed. A low-intensity plyometric is simple in terms of the biomechanical movements in the exercise. A high-intensity plyometric requires a more complex biomechanical action. Measuring the level of intensity in plyometrics is not as exact as it is in resistance training, but the complexity of a movement and its correlation to a specified intensity level gives you a good baseline for measurement.

Volume is another variable in plyometrics. Volume is the total amount of work performed in a given time. The time frame may be a single set, workout, or a longer period of time. In plyometrics, volume refers to the number of times the foot contacts the ground or the number of times the arm extends within a given exercise. Distance is another parameter of volume in plyometrics.

The squat jump is a good example of using foot contact to determine volume. In the squat jump (see page 117), the volume would be measured as the number of times your feet hit the ground during the exercise. When the exercise involves distance, the number of yards an exercise covers is your best measuring device. Again, measurement of volume in plyometrics is not as precise as it is in resistance training.

Another variable in plyometrics is frequency, which is measured the same way as in resistance training. It relates to the number of plyometric workouts performed in a given time frame. The time frame usually used in plyometrics is seven days.

A number of variables come into play when discussing the frequency of plyometric training. Obviously, intensity is one variable. The higher the intensity of a specific plyometric exercise, the less frequently the drill will be performed because of the need for recovery. A minimum of 48 hours between plyometric training sessions is necessary because of the extensive fatigue that results.

Another factor related to the frequency of your training is your stage of martial arts development. A beginner's plyometric training schedule should allow longer periods of rest than an advanced martial artist's schedule. Take a look at tables 7.1 and 7.2, and use them to place your plyometric training into the correct period of frequency. One final note: if you are in a competitive season or are spending extensive time preparing for an upcoming tournament or event, then the number of plyometric sessions per seven-day period should be reduced to one or two at the most.

The final variable of plyometric training is recovery. The purpose of plyometric training is to develop power, speed, and explosive action. The amount of recovery time between sets of plyometrics during a workout has an impact on the overall results of your plyometric training.

Table 7.1   Sample Off-Season (Noncompetitive) Plyometric Programs

Beginner program		Advanced program	
Monday	Thursday	Monday	Thursday
Plyometric knee push-up	Squat jump	Drop and catch push-up	90-second box drill
2-min rest interval	2 sets × 10 reps	2 sets × 10 reps	2 sets
2-min rest interval	2-min rest interval	1-min rest interval	2-min rest interval
Medicine ball seated rotation		Kneeling side throw	Lateral cone hop
2 sets × 10 reps		2 sets × 10 reps	2 sets × 10 reps
2-min rest interval		1-min rest interval	2-min rest interval
		Medicine ball overhead throw	Double-leg tuck jump
		2 sets × 10 reps	2 sets × 10 reps
		1-min rest interval	2-min rest interval

Table 7.2   Sample Frequency of Plyometric Training for Off-Season Training (Noncompetitive)

	Monday	Tuesday	Wednesday	Thursday	Friday
Option 1:					
Beginner/ intermediate	Upper body	None	None	Lower body	None
Option 2:					
Beginner/ intermediate	None	Upper body	None	Lower body	None
Option 3: Advanced	Upper body	Lower body	None	Upper body	Lower body
Option 4: Advanced	Lower body	Upper body	None	Lower body	Upper body

Regardless of the duration (rest time between sets), plyometrics are anaerobic and will develop explosive power in the muscular system. If your rest periods are minimal between sets of plyometric drills, a secondary factor of muscular endurance can be developed in the system. For the development of explosive power from your plyometric training, a work-to-rest ratio of 1:5 to 1:10 is required. This equates to a minimal rest period of two minutes between plyometric sets. A rest period of less than two minutes between sets will result in an additional component of muscular endurance being developed in your system.

So, how should you train with plyometrics? The answer depends on your specific martial art's physical requirements and your individual needs. Let's look at a brief example to get a good understanding. If you participate in a martial art that requires numerous explosive kicks and punches on a continual basis, then it's a good idea to implement plyometric training with a rest period of less than two minutes between sets. This will allow the development of explosive muscular actions along with a secondary development of muscular endurance. On the other hand, if muscular endurance is not a large characteristic of your martial art and your art requires explosive muscular actions, you can put a rest interval (recovery time) of greater than two minutes into your plyometric training.

PLYOMETRIC DRILLS

The following plyometric exercises are classified into beginner, intermediate, and advanced exercises, depending on the neuromuscular difficulty and intensity of the exercise. It is wise to train approximately four to six weeks at each level before advancing to the next level. Table 7.3 lists the drills and equipment you will need.

If you are new to martial arts or resistance training, allow yourself at least 10 to 12 weeks of consistent resistance training before implementing any type of plyometrics into your training. It is better to give yourself more time before starting plyometric training because of the physical demands of plyometric drills.

Beginner Drills

Review tables 7.1 and 7.2 before developing your plyometric protocols. A beginner should implement plyometric drills about two days per week. One session should focus on upper-body plyometrics and the second session should focus on the lower body. Foot contacts for lower-body plyometrics should be between 60 and 100. A maximum of two sets should be performed for each exercise, with a rest period of about two minutes between sets.

Table 7.3 Equipment Needed for Plyometric Drills

Beginner drills

Plyometric drill	Equipment needed
Plyometric knee push-up	None
Medicine ball seated rotation	Medicine ball
Squat jump	None
Split squat	None

Intermediate drills

Plyometric drill	Equipment needed
Medicine ball push-up	Medicine ball
Medicine ball side throw (with partner)	Medicine ball, partner
Double-leg tuck jump	None
Medicine ball overhead throw	Medicine ball

Advanced drills

Plyometric drill	Equipment needed
In-depth push-up	4- to 10-inch box or aerobic step
Kneeling medicine ball throw	Medicine ball
90-second box drill	12-inch box
Lateral cone hop	Cone

PLYOMETRIC KNEE PUSH-UP

Muscles trained: Pectoralis major, deltoids, triceps.

Preparation: Assume a modified push-up position with the knees touching the floor and the ankles crossed. Extend the arms, hands shoulder-width apart. Keep the upper torso and back straight.

Action: Lower your chest to the floor by bending your elbows and rolling slightly forward on your knees. Explosively extend your arms to a straight position, elevating your arms and chest off the floor. Return to the starting position by catching your body when your hands touch the floor. Repeat.

MEDICINE BALL SEATED ROTATION

Muscles trained: Abdominal structure, low back structure, obliques.

Preparation: Sit on the floor with knees slightly bent and heels on the floor. Keep torso at a 45-degree angle from the floor. Grasp a medicine ball in your hands, arms slightly bent.

Action: Starting with the medicine ball on the left side of your body, rotate your torso, shifting the medicine ball to the right side of your body. Maintain a 45-degree torso angle and a slight bend in your elbows. Return to the left side and repeat.

SQUAT JUMP

Muscles trained: Quadriceps, hamstrings, gluteals, hip flexors, hip extensors.

Preparation: Stand with your feet slightly wider than shoulder-width apart, feet flat on the floor, knees bent, hips lowered below knees, back flat, and hands clasped behind head.

Action: Explosively extend your hips up, extending knees to straight position and elevating feet off the floor. Maintain your torso position. Land on the balls of your feet. Absorb the landing by bending your knees and hips. Return to the start position and repeat.

SPLIT SQUAT JUMP

Muscles trained: Quadriceps, hamstrings, hip flexors/extensors, gluteals.

Preparation: Begin in a normal lunge position—left foot in front, right foot in back with the knees slightly bent. The ball of the right foot should be on the ground. Hold your torso upright, arms extended behind shoulder plane, and head facing forward.

Action: Lower your body into deep lunge position with the left knee bending to 90 degrees and right knee bending. Lower torso toward the ground, then forcefully jump up. Drive the arms forward and up. Switch leg positions in the air (right leg to front, left leg to back). Land in opposite lunge position. Absorb landing by bending the knees and lowering the hips toward the floor. Repeat.

Intermediate Drills

After four to six weeks of beginner drills, you may advance to intermediate drills. Intermediate plyometric drills put greater stress on your body, and they are more neuromuscularly challenging. Maintain a schedule of two sessions per seven-day period. Perform two to three sets of each exercise. The number of foot contacts for lower-body exercises should be 100 to 300, and you can vary rest periods depending on your desired outcome.

MEDICINE BALL PUSH-UP

Muscles trained: Pectoralis major, deltoids, triceps.

Preparation: Assume a standard push-up position with your feet six inches apart, toes on the floor, torso straight, back flat, and hands shoulder-width apart. Place the left hand on top of a medicine ball and bend the arms to assume the down position of a push-up.

Action: Forcefully extend the arms straight, shifting laterally in the air to the left. Land with the right hand on top of the medicine ball, left hand on the floor. Absorb the landing by bending the elbows. Repeat the action to the right.

MEDICINE BALL SIDE THROW (WITH PARTNER)

Muscles trained: Low back, abdominal structure, obliques.

Preparation: Stand with your feet shoulder-width apart and knees and elbows slightly bent. Hold a medicine ball to the right side of your body.

Action: Explosively rotate your hips left, throwing the medicine ball to your partner. After completing the hip rotation to the left, allow the arms to extend with the release of the medicine ball. Catch the return throw from your partner. Rotate your hips and torso back to the starting position and repeat.

DOUBLE-LEG TUCK JUMP

Muscles trained: Quadriceps, hamstrings, gluteals, hip flexors and extensors.

Preparation: Stand with your feet flat on the floor slightly wider than shoulder-width apart. Bend your knees to 90 degrees or greater with hips lowered between knees, arms extended behind shoulder plane, and back flat.

Action: Explode up forcefully, jumping off the ground. Bring the knees to a tucked position in front of your chest. Grasp your hands in front of your knees during the tuck portion of the jump. Absorb the landing by bending your ankles, knees, and hips. Return to the starting position and repeat.

MEDICINE BALL OVERHEAD THROW

Muscles trained: Shoulder complex, arm extensors, upper back.

Preparation: Stand with your feet shoulder-width apart, one foot slightly in front of the other, knees slightly bent, torso straight, head forward, arms overhead, and elbows bent. Grasp a medicine ball in both hands behind your head.

Action: Forcefully extend your arms, throwing the medicine ball. Maintain torso and lower body position during the movement. Repeat.

Advanced Drills

After approximately eight weeks of intermediate plyometric drills, you may move on to the advanced drills. Implement the advanced drills into your training two times a week during a noncompetitive period. You will perform two to three sets per exercise. The number of foot contacts for lower-body drills should be 300 to 450 per session. At the advanced stage, you may vary your rest periods between sets and exercises depending on your desired outcome.

IN-DEPTH PUSH-UP

Muscles trained: Pectoralis major, triceps, deltoids.

Preparation: Assume a standard push-up position with your feet together, toes on the ground, back flat, and hands shoulder-width apart. Using a box, aerobic step, or some other flat surface, elevate your hands off the ground 4 to 10 inches, keeping your arms straight.

Action: Lower your body into a normal push-up position. Forcefully straighten your arms, elevating your body. Bring hands close together at the top of the flight portion. Land with your hands on the elevated platform. Absorb the landing by bending your elbows. Repeat.

KNEELING MEDICINE BALL THROW

Muscles trained: Arm extensors, shoulder complex, pectoralis major.

Preparation: Kneel on the ground with your butt tucked under hips and torso leaning forward. Grasp a medicine ball in both hands at chest level. Keep your arms bent.

Action: Forcefully throw the ball from the chest at a 45-degree angle from the floor, extending arms, torso, and legs simultaneously. Catch your body on the floor in a push-up position. Return to starting position and repeat.

90-SECOND BOX DRILL

Muscles trained: Calves, quadriceps, hamstrings, hip extensors, gluteals.

Preparation: Place a 12-inch box on the floor. Stand about six inches away from the box with your feet shoulder-width apart, feet flat on the floor, knees slightly bent, torso slightly leaning forward, and elbows bent.

Action: Jump onto the box in a rapid motion, driving arms forward and extending the knees slightly during the jump. Land on top of the box. Return to the starting position and repeat the jump as quickly as possible. Continue to jump for 90 seconds.

LATERAL CONE HOP

Muscles trained: Calves, quadriceps, hamstrings, hip flexors and extensors, gluteals.

Preparation: Stand to the left side of a cone with the knees slightly bent, feet flat and close together, elbows bent, and torso leaning slightly forward.

Action: Jump sideways over the cone, extending your knees and ankles. Extend your arms forward. Land on the right side of the cone and immediately jump to the left side of the cone. Repeat jumps as rapidly as possible. Perform a set of 10 to 25 jumps, or jump for 30 to 60 seconds.

SUMMARY

This chapter has provided a detailed explanation of the benefits of plyometrics and how to implement them into your training program. Let's review a few guidelines to follow when implementing these drills.

- Develop a sound base of strength through resistance training before implementing plyometric drills into your fitness program.
- Perform a proper warm-up before beginning plyometric drills.
- Combine lower-body strength training with upper-body plyometrics, and upper-body strength training with lower-body plyometrics (see table 7.4).
- Allow 48 to 72 hours of recovery between plyometric sessions.
- Follow a proper progression from beginner to intermediate to advanced plyometric drills.

Keep these principles in mind when developing and implementing plyometric drills. Maintain proper safety, form, and procedure for each drill, and your plyometric training will add speed, power, and quickness to your martial arts techniques.

Table 7.4 Sample Core Exercise Resistance Training/Plyometric Schedule for Beginners

Monday	Wednesday	Friday
Multijoint/single-joint exercises	Multijoint/single-joint exercises	Multijoint/single-joint exercises
Upper-body plyometrics	Aerobic/anaerobic drills	Lower-body plyometrics

CHAPTER 8

AEROBIC AND ANAEROBIC CONDITIONING

Optimal performance in the martial arts requires a certain level of aerobic conditioning. For example, when you perform a series of katas or sparring rounds, you will find yourself breathing more heavily than you do during your day-to-day activities. The heavy breathing is a sign that you are asking more out of your body in the form of aerobic and anaerobic output. You may achieve a higher level of performance when your aerobic and anaerobic capacities are enhanced. Proper training of your aerobic and anaerobic output will result in less fatigue during practice and competition and an improvement in overall performance. This chapter covers the specifics of aerobic and anaerobic capacities and how to improve them to benefit your performance in the martial arts.

AEROBIC CONDITIONING

Aerobic conditioning is the process of putting oxygen into the body. The goal of aerobic conditioning is not to increase your oxygen uptake, or $\dot{V}O_2$max; anaerobic conditioning does that. Aerobic exercise moves oxygen through the body. For this reason, the intensity at which you perform aerobic training is very important. A good guideline to ensure that you are working out at a good intensity is the talk test: you should be able to carry on a normal conversation when performing aerobic activities. This will help you work at a proper intensity to reach the goals of your aerobic training.

The duration and frequency of aerobic training ranges from 25 to 45 minutes per session, three to six sessions per week. This broad range allows flexibility in incorporating your conditioning program into your overall martial arts training. The amount of aerobic training you need will depend on where you are in your martial arts training (competitive period, precompetitive period, or off-season). Allow the other facets of training and your stage in the competitive cycle to determine the frequency and duration of aerobic training.

ANAEROBIC CONDITIONING

The process, outcome, and variables associated with anaerobic training are completely different than those of aerobic conditioning. The goal of anaerobic training is to improve the oxygen uptake of your cardiovascular system (measured uniformly by your $\dot{V}O_2$max). Let's consider an example of anaerobic activity in the martial arts and define it in more depth.

During physically strenuous activities, your muscles require oxygen and nutrients to function. If you were performing a series of two-minute sparring rounds in muay thai, you would probably find yourself breathing very heavily between rounds and at the end of the session. This is because your muscles are screaming for oxygen so that they can maintain function during this vigorous bout of activity. This example also illustrates that when you breathe heavily to get oxygen into your system, your body performs less than optimally. If you improve the delivery of oxygen and nutrients to your working muscles, fatigue will set in later, recovery between rigorous exercise bouts will occur more quickly, speed and agility will improve, and overall performance will be enhanced.

These are the four goals of anaerobic training:

- Increase the amount of oxygen delivered to working muscles and the rate at which it is delivered
- Decrease the rate at which muscular fatigue sets in during vigorous physical activity
- Decrease recovery time between exercise bouts
- Increase speed and agility

Before covering the specific drills, we'll look at the parameters of setting up anaerobic drills.

Training Parameters

Before beginning any series of anaerobic drills, perform a proper warm-up with flexibility work to raise your body's core temperature. Because of the explosive muscular nature of these drills, a warm-up is necessary to decrease your chance of injury.

During a noncompetitive period in your training, you can do anaerobic training three to four days per week. During a competitive period, reduce anaerobic training to one to two days per week. The number of anaerobic drills you perform in a single session will be determined by the training experience you have.

Rest for about one minute between sets. The purpose of these drills is to improve $\dot{V}O_2$max, and the only way to do that is to place your body in oxygen deficit. The order of your training session would be as follows: warm-up, flexibility work, torso work, joint-stabilization exercises, resistance training, anaerobic drills, and plyometrics. It is best to place anaerobic drills after resistance training and before plyometrics because of muscular fatigue. Better yet, set aside separate training sessions for anaerobic training.

Following are a series of anaerobic drills to integrate into your martial arts training. The exercises not only relate to specific movements in the martial arts, but they also meet the goal of anaerobic training: to improve your $\dot{V}O_2$max, which will result in the benefits listed earlier.

INTERVAL SPRINTS

Preparation: For the Interval Sprints and the Sprint/Jog Intervals described later, you may want to run on a track. A running track provides a good running surface and will help you keep track of your intervals since it is premeasured.

Action: For the Interval Sprints, you will alternate between sprinting (running as fast as you can) and walking. Begin with the sprint. Sprint for 25 yards, then walk for one minute. Sprint another 25 yards and walk for one minute. Continue alternating sprinting and walking until you've completed one mile.

HILL SPRINTS

Preparation: Find a flat running surface with a 1 to 3 degree incline. Mark start and finish lines 20 yards apart.

Action: Sprint up the incline, running as fast as you can for 20 yards. Return to the start line. Rest for one minute between sets. Perform 2 to 3 sets.

SPRINT/JOG INTERVALS

Preparation: As with the Interval Sprints described earlier, you may want to run Sprint/Jog Intervals on a running track. A running track provides a good running surface and will help you keep track of your intervals since it is premeasured.

Action: For the Sprint/Jog Intervals, you will alternate between sprinting (running as fast as you can) and jogging. Begin with the sprint. Sprint for 25 yards, then jog for one minute. Sprint another 25 yards and jog for one minute. Continue alternating sprinting and jogging until you've completed one mile.

FOUR-CORNER CARIOCA DRILL

Preparation: Set up four cones in a box shape, with 10 to 15 yards between cones, depending on your level of conditioning.

Action: Stand to the right of the first cone. Step toward the second cone with your left foot over your right foot. Move your right foot behind your left foot. Again step your left foot in front of your right foot. Continue toward the second cone. When you reach the second cone, turn sideways toward the third cone. Continue around the box until you return to the first cone. Rest for one minute. Repeat, moving the other way around the box, with your right foot stepping in front of your left foot.

CONE ZIG-ZAG

Preparation: Set up 10 cones in a straight line, with one yard between each cone.

Action: Step forward with your right foot to the right of the first cone. Slide your left foot to your right foot. Step forward with your left foot to the left of the second cone. Slide your right foot to your left foot. Continue to zigzag through the cones. Remember to move quickly and explosively. Rest for one minute between sets. Perform 2 to 3 sets.

SUMMARY

Aerobic and anaerobic training enhance performance in the martial arts. Aerobic training leads to a greater rate of recovery between workout sessions, and when combined with proper nutrition, may help you lose a few pounds. Anaerobic training develops $\dot{V}O_2$max and also improves your speed and agility. Even though aerobic and anaerobic training is more general than specific to the style of martial art you practice, the benefits will cross over into advancement and performance in your art. Training the body with activities that are not directly related to your martial art—sprints, for example—will still improve your development in your martial art.

CHAPTER 9

NUTRITION AND RECOVERY

We've discussed training principles

and specific exercises in previous chapters. The process of preparing your body for competition through martial arts classes, tournaments, and presentations is only one facet in the big picture of optimal success. Proper nutrition, recovery, and supplementation are also necessary to optimize your success in the martial arts. This chapter looks at all three of these variables. Before moving to nutrition, let's look at how your repair cycle (the recovery time between training sessions), nutrition, and supplementation work together to achieve results.

THE CIRCLE OF SUCCESS

Performance analyst Tom House has devised the proper combination of physical preparation (prepare) and recovery, nutrition, and supplementation (repair) for success in competition (see figure 9.1). After a class, tournament, or presentation—identified as your competitive period—you must allow your body to repair itself with proper rest, nutrition, and supplementation. After a repair cycle, you can resume a cycle of preparing the body (resistance training, flexibility work, joint-stabilization work) to obtain a higher level of fitness for competition. It comes down to a cycle of repair, prepare, compete.

This cycle (or circle of success) illustrates a few ideas. First, at any given time you are in one of these three positions in the circle. You are either competing, repairing, or preparing the body for the stresses placed on it by the martial arts. Second, the circle illustrates that training is cyclical in nature. Your body continually moves through these stages as you progress through the martial arts on a day-to-day, week-to-week, month-to-month

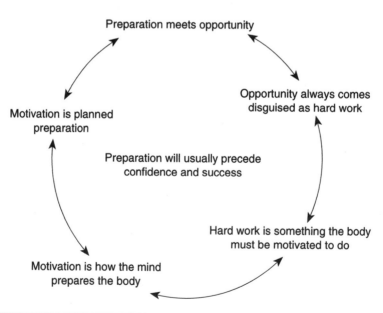

Figure 9.1 The circle of success.

Reprinted, by permission, from Tom House, 2000, *The Pitching Edge*, 2nd ed. (Champaign, IL: Human Kinetics).

basis. Finally, each of the three stages (compete, repair, and prepare) holds the same weight of importance. No one category is more important than another; they all work together to place you in a position of optimal success.

All the concepts presented to this point are functions in developing you as a martial artist. This chapter focuses on nutrition, which is an element of the repair portion of the circle of success.

MACRONUTRIENTS

You have probably heard the basics of what fuels your body: carbohydrates, fats, and proteins. All three of these components are used for a variety of functions. Carbohydrates, fats, and proteins can be classified as macronutrients. Macronutrients are present in the foods you eat and they provide you with energy. The majority of these nutrients are digested in the stomach and broken down into amino acids, simple sugars, and fat molecules to be absorbed in the bloodstream and used for energy. The body generally uses carbohydrates (sugars) first, fats second, and proteins (amino acids) third for energy. Fats supply slightly more than twice the amount of energy per gram than carbohydrates do. The utilization of these nutrients depends on the secretion of hormones, which facilitate the use of these nutrients in cellular activity.

The body responds to existing circumstances. For example, if you ingest a large amount of carbohydrates, a large amount of insulin is released from the pancreas. If you eat a large amount of protein, your system will increase production of glucagon. Your body regulates the amount of enzymes secreted by your cells to compensate for the food you digest. Your body is smart if you just let it be.

You need to be aware of the proper ratio of carbohydrates, fats, and proteins for optimal martial arts performance. Let's address a few misconceptions and discuss the principles of proper nutrient intake.

Carbohydrate loading.   Research done by Dr. Richard Hietsch of the Human Performance Group suggests that carbohydrate loading benefits only untrained athletes. An athlete who has been training consistently, allowing his or her body to gear up for activity at a cellular level, will use all three essential nutrients—carbohydrates, fats, and proteins—effectively as sources of energy, thereby generating more total energy for a longer period of time. Gearing up at a cellular level—using carbohydrates, fat, and proteins optimally—enhances physical performance because the body is able to use all three sources of energy efficiently.

Carbohydrate loading is only one example of the many fallacies circulating about the proper ratios of carbohydrates, fats, and proteins needed to provide the body with energy. So, what is the proper ratio of carbohydrate, fat, and protein for optimal recovery and long-term health? A ratio of 40 percent carbohydrate, 30 to 40 percent protein, and 20 to 30 percent fat appears to be the optimal healthy balance. Also important is the type of foods within these categories, especially fat and carbohydrate. Processed or refined carbohydrate such as sugar should be avoided, while complex carbohydrates such as those found in fresh fruits and vegetables should be a diet staple. Processed fat such as margarine should be avoided in favor of natural fat such as olive oil. In general, natural fat is healthier than processed fat, but keep in mind that we all need some dietary fat for health.

Fiber.   Another area that has received a great deal of attention recently is fiber. Fiber has many functions in the body, particularly when it comes to digestion. The healthiest type of carbohydrate is referred to as high-fiber carbohydrate. Consume high-fiber carbohydrates from vine-ripened fresh fruits and vegetables. Avoid processed carbohydrate such as sugary cereals, white bread, and candy.

Protein.   Protein can be derived from either plants or animals. In some people, certain protein sources can cause adverse reactions such as an upset stomach, so be aware of your sensitivities when choosing your source of protein. Choose natural sources of protein (plant or animal), and avoid any food sensitivities you may have, such as lactose intolerance from dairy sources. Be sure to get enough protein in your diet (20 to 30 percent of your total calories) relative to carbohydrate intake to balance out glucagon secretion and insulin production.

Food combining.   How you eat may also be important in your quest for optimal health. Some have heralded food combining as a useful dietary tool. The theory behind food combining is that consuming large amounts of protein and carbohydrate in a single meal puts the digestive process into a tailspin, so to speak.

Protein takes longer to digest than carbohydrate, and the majority of this digestive process takes place in the stomach. Carbohydrate, on the other hand, begins the digestion process in the mouth through salivation and is broken down and absorbed very quickly. By combining protein and carbohydrate in a single meal, you expose a large amount of the digested carbohydrate to acidic conditions in the stomach, resulting in fermentation rather than digestion. Research done by Dr. Richard Hietsch of the Human Performance Group suggests that this results in a less than optimal use of the carbohydrate you consumed for energy. Therefore, the theory of food combining suggests that it is best to emphasize either protein or carbohydrate at a single meal rather than combining them.

Another idea is that eating patterns are predicated on different blood types. At this time, there is no concrete data to support this idea.

Let's cover a few more points about macronutrients before exploring micronutrients. The general goal of nutritional management is to support your work/play environment. Proper nutritional intake should match the required needs of your physical output. In other words, eat to fuel your body for the needs of your daily activities.

Food combining and food rotating may help you achieve a proper balance between blood chemistry and physical output. We discussed food combining earlier. The idea behind food rotating is to not eat the same food prepared the same way twice in a 72-hour period. This mix 'n' match approach to eating may help you avoid food sensitivities and allow for optimal digestion of the foods you consume.

Keeping these two ideas in mind will help you optimize your eating for your daily activities and the martial arts. Think of eating the same way you think of training. Eat specific to the activities you are to participate in on a daily basis.

MICRONUTRIENTS

Macronutrients also supply fuel that allows your body to function. Micronutrients are the secondary piece of the puzzle in metabolic management. In general, micronutrients are needed only in small amounts, but without them the body cannot produce the chemicals necessary to maintain optimal functioning. Many of the micronutrients we will discuss are cofactors that help chemical reactions in the body occur at a faster rate. For example, the minerals zinc and magnesium are necessary in more than 300 chemical reactions in the body, while vitamin C is needed to maintain the integrity of collagen structures in your body and vitamin K is needed for blood clotting. These examples give you a good idea of how micronutrients function in the body and how important they are to your blood chemistry and general functioning.

The actual amount of micronutrients needed continues to be debated. The important point to remember is that at the least, a minimal amount is needed by the body to allow for chemical reactions within your system. Supplementation of daily food intake may be necessary to make sure you obtain the proper amounts of certain dietary agents.

Before we list the suggested supplements, review a few important points about supplementation. First, make sure the nutrients supplied by supplements are high in bioavailability. If you ingest supplements that the body cannot readily use, then the supplements are useless in helping you reach your dietary objectives. It is important to use high-quality supplements that provide nutrients in a form your body can readily dissolve and absorb. Second, watch for quantity. Some dietary supplements cost more than others, and some supplements lack needed micronutrients. A correlation often exists between price and the quantity of micronutrients in a supplement. When adding supplements, make sure you do not miss any important nutrients.

The list that follows contains the micronutrients I suggest for optimal blood chemistry. Remember to follow the points described previously and add supplements to your daily routine for optimal metabolic functioning.

- Comprehensive vitamin-mineral complex
- Broad-based antioxidant formula
- Essential fatty acid supplement (dietary need for omega 3 and omega 6)
- Digestive enzyme supplement (helps break down protein and fat)

In the sample diet shown in table 9.1, the principles of food combining and food rotating are used. You also may want to consider food supplementation. When should you take supplements? If you have stomach sensitivities, it may be best to take dietary supplements in the middle of your largest meal. This allows for proper digestion of the supplements, protecting your stomach and allowing for the greatest utilization of these supplements by your body.

Table 9.1 Sample Five-Day Eating Plan

	Day 1	Day 2	Day 3	Day 4	Day 5
Breakfast	1 cup oatmeal or dry cereal 1 cup skim milk Banana Whole wheat bagel	3 pancakes 3 egg whites 3 tbsp. lowfat syrup 1 cup of fruit	1 cup oatmeal 3 egg whites Orange	1 cup oatmeal or dry cereal 1 cup skim milk Banana Whole wheat bagel	French toast 3 tbsp. lowfat syrup Piece of fruit

Morning snack	Piece of fruit	8 oz. yogurt with nonfat lowfat granola	Lowfat bran muffin	Orange	None
Lunch	Turkey sandwich on 2 slices of whole wheat bread Glass of water	Tuna salad sandwich made with 1 tbsp. nonfat mayonnaise on a bagel Glass of water	Turkey sandwich made with 1 tbsp. nonfat mayonnaise on a pita 1 cup steamed vegetables Glass	Chicken salad sandwich made with 1 tbsp. nonfat mayonnaise on whole wheat bread Glass of water	Turkey sandwich made with 1 tbsp. nonfat mayonnaise on rye bread Large green salad Glass of water
Afternoon snack	Lowfat bran muffin	Piece of fruit	2 bananas	Egg bagel	Lowfat bran muffin
Dinner	1 whole chicken breast 1 cup steamed vegetables Small mixed-greens dinner salad with 1 tbsp. vinegar and olive oil dressing	Turkey meatballs made with lean ground turkey 1 cup pasta Large dinner salad	Grilled fish filet 1 cup steamed vegetables Small dinner salad	Grilled turkey breast 1 small potato Dinner salad	Shrimp scampi cooked in olive oil 1 cup rice 1 cup steamed vegetables Dinner salad
Evening snack	None	None	Celery and carrot sticks	1 cup yogurt and fruit	None

REST AND RECOVERY

The majority of this chapter is geared toward nutrition. A second element in developing an optimal recovery program between workouts is rest. Rest can be divided into two areas: the rest time between sets during resistance training and the rest time between exercise bouts. Proper rest and recovery, combined with sound nutrition, prepares your body for optimal performance in the martial arts.

Recovery Between Sets

The first area of rest we will discuss is recovery time between sets or exercises, or the microcycle. Recovery time between sets or exercises is determined by the specificity of your training. Are you training for muscular power, strength, or endurance?

Rest periods within a microcycle are critical to the outcome of resistance training. For example, if you want to develop more muscular endurance to maintain proper technique during sparring matches, resting two to three minutes between sets will not develop the muscular endurance you want. This is too much rest between sets.

Let's break down how to determine what your rest periods should be. Your rest period between sets will be determined based on your training goal. Review table 9.2 to determine the proper rest period between sets for specific variable development. Keep in mind that muscles can be trained specifically for power, strength, endurance, and balance. This table also gives the proper intensity level, repetition ratio, and workout frequency in the microcycle.

You can see from table 9.2 that the rest interval (recovery time) has a large influence on the outcome of training. Review the parameters of your martial art (muscular endurance, power, strength, or a combination) and plan the correct rest intervals between sets during your workouts.

Recovery Between Workouts

Another element of recovery deals with macrocycle recovery intervals—the rest period between resistance-training sessions. Let's look at a few parameters that determine the amount of time specific muscles or groups of muscles need to recover for optimal functioning.

Table 9.2 Training Variables (Microcycle)

Type of training	Load and intensity	Pre-set repetition level	Rest period between sets	Workout frequency (times per week)
Strength/ hypertrophy	70–90%	6–12	30–60 sec	4
Endurance	70% or more	15 or more	Less than 30 sec	2–6
Power	90% or less	5 or less	2–3 min	2–3
Balance	90% or more	6 or more	2 min or less	2–6

Muscle size is a determining factor when setting up your macrocycle. A general principle to follow is that small muscles (rotator cuff, biceps, triceps) need less time to rest between training sessions than do large muscles (chest, back, quadriceps). Small muscles can be trained with 24 hours between training sessions. Large muscles, on the other hand, need a recovery time of 48 to 72 hours between intense training sessions for optimal recovery. As with microcycle recovery intervals, macrocycle rest periods should be geared toward the goals of your resistance program and the requirements of your martial art. Use this information to help complete your training program.

SUMMARY

The information in this chapter will help you with your repair stage. Remember the circle of success introduced at the beginning of this chapter: repair, prepare, compete. The repair process is just as important as what you do to prepare for the martial arts. Pay attention to your nutrition and recovery, using your goals to focus both. This will result in optimal gains and performance. One final note: listen to your body. Your body will tell you what is going right or wrong when you're preparing and repairing your body for the martial arts. Your body is smart if you let it be.

CHAPTER 10

DESIGNING YOUR CONDITIONING PROGRAM

Now it is time to bring together all

the information from chapters 1 through 9. This chapter presents guidelines to design, implement, and alter your workout program as you progress in your training and your martial art. When reading this chapter, keep in mind the information presented earlier and refer to previous chapters when necessary. Now you will design a training program specific to your goals and the physical requirements of your martial art.

Before beginning your training program, you must determine the goals and parameters of your training. For example, if you find that you lack the muscular power for takedown techniques in judo, then you will gear some of your training toward developing muscular power. We will review resistance-training programs for beginning through advanced levels. People with a strong background in resistance training may choose the programs and techniques that work best for them. Remember to specify your training to the requirements of your martial art.

PROGRAM DESIGN

Everyone will have different goals, exercises, and variables within their training programs. Because of this, the first step in any resistance-training program is determining your personal needs. The second step is to develop a training program that meets those needs. Begin with a "needs analysis"—a review of your strong and weak points—then determine your training goals based on your needs. You must invest a little time at the beginning or else you will find yourself putting in a great deal of time and effort but achieving less-than-optimal results.

Needs Analysis and Training Goals

A needs analysis essentially entails determining what requirements your training program must meet. Two areas to focus on when preparing your needs analysis are specificity and the physical requirements of your martial art. Plan to train specifically to the movements and athletic requirements of your martial art. When you begin your needs analysis, review your martial art and determine the physical requirements and biomechanics of the martial art. This information will help you determine the muscular, aerobic, anaerobic, and biomechanical emphasis for your training schedule.

Your needs analysis also will help you find the areas that need improvement. For example, if you lack muscular endurance in the lower body and your martial art requires muscular endurance in the lower body, then a key area of your training should be the development of muscular endurance in the legs and torso. Although overall your analysis aims to develop a map of the specific physical requirements of your art, it also will highlight areas that require improvement.

The next step is to map out your training goals. Once you have determined what you need, develop a list of goals for your training program. A single goal may be the focus of your entire training program or your may have a combination of goals. Here are some sample goals:

- Improved flexibility
- Increased muscular endurance
- Greater muscle hypertrophy
- Improved muscular power
- Better muscle balance

As you can see, your training program can be fine-tuned to the needs of your martial art and your goals. This brings you to the point of setting up your training program. Most training programs follow a specified sequence.

Order of Resistance Training

An ideal resistance-training schedule follows this sequence:

1. General warm-up
2. Flexibility exercises
3. Torso-stabilization exercises
4. Joint-stabilization exercises
5. Core exercises
6. Anaerobic training
7. Plyometric training
8. Aerobic training

This sequence allows for the proper ratios of flexibility, joint stabilization, torso stabilization, and resistance exercises for improvement in the martial arts. Further information on each of these areas follows.

General Warm-Up

A general warm-up raises your core temperature a few degrees and prepares your muscular system for the stresses that will be placed on it throughout your program. The main focus is to warm up the body, do some flexibility exercises, and get the body ready to work. A warm-up may consist of a variety of activities, such as jogging, riding a stationary bike, jogging on a treadmill, or any other aerobic activity that raises the core body temperature.

Flexibility Exercises

After completing a general warm-up, move into flexibility exercises. More information on flexibility exercises is found in chapter 3. Remember to perform flexibility work before any resistance training exercises or martial arts practice. The goals of these exercises are

1. to provide a "wake-up call" to all tissues in your muscular system,
2. to improve the range of motion about your joints, and
3. to increase the flexibility of your muscular system.

Torso-Stabilization Exercises

Now move to torso-stabilization exercises (see chapter 5). These exercises provide a complete strengthening program for the abdomen and lower back through the use of flexibility, isometric, and medicine ball exercises. Remember that a lack of torso strength will decrease your ability to develop rotational torque, maintain balance, and execute techniques correctly.

Joint-Stabilization Exercises

Joint-stabilization exercises are next (see chapter 4). These exercises use elastic cords, bodywork, and light dumbbells to develop balance within the muscular system. Remember that muscular balance is the development of a systematic ratio or equality between small muscles and tissues around skeletal joints and large primary movers. This ratio or equality pertains to the development of muscular strength and endurance within the system. A lack of balance between these large and small tissues can result in injury and a decline in performance.

Core Exercises

At this point, you are ready to start your core exercise program. The exercises you add on at this point depend on your goals, the requirements of your martial art, and your training experience. Design your core exercise program with these factors in mind.

Core exercises should revolve around the principle of multijoint and single-joint exercises. Multijoint exercises require the movement of more than one joint, which in turn recruit more muscles. Single-joint exercises require a range of motion from one joint, which in turn recruit fewer muscles. For example, a power clean (see page 90) recruits the ankle, knee, hip, and shoulder joints into the movement. Therefore, a power clean is a multijoint exercise. A biceps barbell curl requires only the elbow joint. This exercise is a single-joint exercise. The golden rule for core exercises is to perform multijoint exercises before single-joint exercises (see chapter 6).

Anaerobic Training

After core exercises, add anaerobic exercises to your program. The goal of these exercises is to increase $\dot{V}O_2$max allowing a greater intake of oxygen into your system. An increase in $\dot{V}O_2$max will increase the rate and amount of oxygen delivered to working muscles, decrease fatigue factors, and decrease recovery time (see chapter 8 for further information). Keep in mind that you should not do anaerobic work every day. Plan anaerobic training for two to four days per week depending on where you are in your training (off-season, precompetitive, competitive period).

Plyometric Training

Plyometric drills are next. The goal of plyometrics is to develop rapid and explosive actions from your muscles, which help you develop a greater rate of force production and contractile speed. Because plyometrics cause muscular fatigue, they should be performed toward the end of your training program. If you attempt to perform anaerobic activities or other drills in a state of muscular fatigue, the benefits from such exercises will be diminished greatly.

Aerobic Training

The last facet of your training program is aerobic training. Aerobic activities focus on supplying your muscles with oxygen and nutrients that aid the recovery process and help with fat loss. Aerobic activities facilitate the repair of muscle tissue. Therefore you should always perform aerobic activities last because your muscles will undergo tissue repair during aerobic exercise. The frequency of aerobic activity depends on your training stage, but plan to engage in aerobic exercise two to six days a week.

This sequence gives you an outline to follow when developing your martial arts training program. Remember to use the information from your needs analysis and train specifically to the requirements of your martial art.

GENERAL CONDITIONING PROGRAM

A general conditioning program is ideal for anyone new to resistance training or just beginning in the martial arts. Plan to spend the first 8 to 12 weeks in the general conditioning program before moving to the next step. A period of 8 to 12 weeks will allow your body to develop physically and prepare you for a more advanced program.

Be sure to follow the correct program sequence, beginning with a general warm-up, moving through core exercises, and finishing with anaerobic and aerobic activities. You will not perform any plyometrics until you reach an advanced stage of training because of the neuromuscular requirements of plyometric activities. The general conditioning program ends with core exercises and includes a couple of days of aerobic and anaerobic training.

Over time you will begin to notice changes in your body composition, strength, stamina, flexibility, and martial arts performance. Most beginners notice that they are more comfortable using the weights after a short period of time as the neuromuscular system adjusts to the new movements. This should be evident after the first four weeks.

The general conditioning program is a typical program for the beginning martial artist. This program uses exercises presented in previous chapters.

Frequency: Three times per week.

Program Outline

1. Warm-up
2. Flexibility exercises (chapter 3)
3. Torso-stabilization exercises (chapter 5)
4. Joint-stabilization exercises (chapter 4)
5. Core exercises (chapter 6)
6. Anaerobic training (chapter 8)
7. Aerobic training (chapter 8)

Flexibility Exercises

1. Calf Stretch
2. Seated Groin Stretch
3. Thigh Lunge
4. Side Quad Flex
5. Single-Arm Side Bend
6. Supermans (Alternating Arms)
7. Back Flexion
8. Back Extension
9. Neck Side to Side
10. Arm Cross

Torso-Stabilization Exercises

1. Low Back Press
2. Single-Leg Low Back Raise

3. Supermans (Both Arms)

4. Abdominal Crunches

5. Abdominal Side Crunches

Joint-Stabilization Exercises

1. Butt-Ups

2. Flex-T Push-Ups

3. One-Arm Side-Ups

4. Shoulder Circles

5. Internal Rotation

6. External Rotation

7. Reverse Rotators

Circuit training: One exercise per body part, 10 to 15 repetitions per exercise. Complete a single set per exercise.

Core Exercises

1. Dumbbell Bench Press

2. Deadlift

3. Lunges

4. Lat Pulldown

5. Biceps Barbell Curl

6. Triceps Cable Extension

Anaerobic Training

Interval Sprints.

Aerobic Training

Ride a stationary bike for 25 minutes two times per week.

INTERMEDIATE CONDITIONING PROGRAM

The intermediate conditioning program is the next step if you are advancing through a series of resistance-training programs. If you have been involved in the martial arts for some time and have some experience in resistance training (at least three months), this is an ideal place to start. If you have been successfully using the general conditioning program described in the previous section for 8 to 12 weeks, you should be ready to move to the intermediate program.

In the intermediate conditioning program, your exercises will become more specific to your martial art. You should do a needs analysis so that your training will be specific to your goals. Before looking at the intermediate conditioning program, let's look at some new principles you will find in this program.

Resistance-Training Principles

At this point you have a sound base of information to use to implement your martial arts resistance-training program. You have been presented with a general conditioning program and are ready to start training more specifically for your martial art. The seven training principles that follow will advance your program by implementing greater workloads on your body. Most of these principles pertain to core exercises, but you also will find them useful when setting up your entire training program. The principles to be discussed are periodization, split routine, cycling, heavy-light, supersets, tri-sets, and pyramiding.

All seven of these principles are beneficial to the intermediate or advanced athlete looking to make greater strides in his or her martial arts and resistance training. Overall, the increased volume and intensity of these programs increase the workload on your muscular system. These principles will provide continual gains in your training program.

Periodization

Periodization was discussed briefly in chapter 1 (see page 10). Let's review this principle and add to it. Periodization is the cycling of load, volume, intensity, and exercises in a given time period. The time frame may be divided into days, weeks, months, or years. Each time frame has a specific arrangement of load, volume, intensity, and exercises. Cycles can be broken into macrocycles and mesocycles.

A macrocycle is the complete training time, which is usually one year. A mesocycle is a specific part of the macrocycle (for example, one season). Usually, the mesocycle is planned around certain important competitions or events. To further illustrate a mesocycle, let's look at an example from weightlifting. If you were planning to compete in a powerlifting contest in which you performed a bench press, you would cycle your bench-press training within the macrocycle (the year) and schedule a mesocycle around this event. The mesocycle itself can be broken into phases (for example, one week) according to the general plan of your training.

Here are the subdivisions of the mesocycle:

1. Phase 1: hypertrophy and endurance training. The body gains muscular endurance and hypertrophy.

2. Phase 2: strength training. The body improves its strength. Intensity increases, but overall volume decreases.

3. Phase 3: power/sport-specific training. Sport-specific movements are refined, and the athlete focuses on a specific season or event (for example, a competitive bodybuilding show). The athlete will focus and refine training for this specific event.

4. Phase 4: competition/maintenance training. Intensity is lower and volume is decreased so that the person can focus on the sport he or she is competing in. Phase 4 also can be a time for the athlete to get some active rest before beginning another cycle. (Active rest involves participating in other recreational activities besides weight training and martial arts.)

Periodization provides many benefits to your training. It allows you to focus your training on a certain event or sport. It also places planned recovery times in your program. Continual training at maximum intensity and load will diminish your gains and decrease your performance. Periodization allows the body to gradually adapt to new stresses placed on it. It also allows you to peak at the correct time for a specific event.

Split Routine

Based on a principle made popular by Boyd Epley at the University of Nebraska and implemented by athletes at that school, the split system divides the muscles of the body and trains them on different days. The advantage to such a program is that it uses shorter workouts, allows certain muscles to recover while other muscles are working, and permits the person to compete in other activities while weight training without becoming fatigued. The split system also allows you to implement other training principles—such as multijoint, single-joint, or plyometric exercises—into your training program. A sample split system program for a martial artist could look like this:

- *Monday:* Warm-up, flexibility exercises, joint-stabilization exercises, torso-stabilization exercises, multijoint exercises, single-joint exercises, aerobic training.

- *Tuesday:* Warm-up, flexibility exercises, martial arts practice, anaerobic training, plyometric exercises.

- *Wednesday:* Warm-up, flexibility exercises, joint-stabilization exercises, torso-stabilization exercises, multijoint exercises, single-joint exercises, aerobic training.
- *Thursday:* Warm-up, flexibility exercises, martial arts practice, anaerobic training, plyometric exercises.
- *Friday:* Warm-up, flexibility exercises, joint-stabilization exercises, torso-stabilization exercises, multijoint exercises, single-joint exercises, aerobic training.
- *Saturday:* Warm-up, flexibility exercises, martial arts practice, aerobic training.
- *Sunday:* Rest.

Cycling

Another advanced training technique used at the University of Nebraska and many other collegiate and professional institutions is cycling. This principle prevents overtraining and progressively pushes the body to greater strength, endurance, and power gains. The idea behind the principle is to change the intensity and volume of an exercise from set to set and from workout to workout. This keeps the body from stagnating and falling into detraining. Cycling works well with periodization. Table 10.1 shows how a core exercise—the bench press—would be used with the cycling principle within a periodization schedule.

You can see how well the two concepts of periodization and cycling fit together. Using cycling within a periodization program will elicit greater gains in muscular endurance and hypertrophy, strength, and power. It will also prevent you from overtraining or going into detraining. Remember, always schedule your resistance training around your martial arts practice time. Do not let resistance training override classroom training time.

Heavy-Light

Another principle from Boyd Epley is called the heavy-light system, which fits into the principles of split routine and cycling. This system revolves around heavily training each body part one time a week, then training with a light workout the second training period within a seven-day time frame. The goal of the heavy-light system is to elicit the greatest gains in strength, endurance, and power, and limit the risk of overtraining. The heavy-light system plans heavy workouts as the first workouts in the week with light workouts as the second set in the week. What follows is an example of a heavy-light program during phase 2 (strength) of a periodization schedule. The repetition and intensity levels in table 10.2 refer to the core exercises only.

Table 10.1   Example of Cycling: Bench Press Within a Periodization Cycle

Phase/set	Repetitions	Intensity
Phase 1 Endurance/hypertrophy		
Set 1	12	60%
Set 2	12	65%
Set 3	12	70%
Phase 2 Strength		
Set 1	6	75%
Set 2	6	80%
Set 3	6	85%
Phase 3 Power/sport specific		
Set 1	3	85%
Set 2	3	87%
Set 3	3	90%
Phase 4 Competition/maintenance		
Set 1	10	65%
Set 2	10	70%
Set 3	10	70%

- Monday: Flexibility work, torso work, joint stabilization, core exercises (power cleans, push press, shoulder press, biceps barbell curl).
- Tuesday: Flexibility work, torso work, joint stabilization, core exercises (squats, bench press, leg curls, triceps cable pressdowns).
- Thursday: Flexibility work, torso work, joint stabilization, core exercises (power cleans, push press, shoulder press, biceps barbell curl).
- Friday: Flexibility work, torso work, joint stabilization, core exercises (squats, bench press, leg curls, triceps cable pressdowns).

Both the volume of work and the intensity change. This allows for maximum gains in the phase and, more importantly, lessens the risk of injury and overtraining.

Table 10.2   Intensity and Volume for Sample Heavy-Light Program (Core Exercises Only)

	Repetitions	Intensity
Monday/Tuesday		
Set 1	8	70%
Set 2	8	72%
Set 3	8	75%
Thursday/Friday		
Set 1	8	70%
Set 2	8	70%

Supersets

A superset consists of alternating between two exercises with little or no rest between each set. The superset may involve two exercises for the same body part, or it may involve exercises for opposing agonist and antagonist muscles. The theory behind this principle is that reducing the time between sets and adding to the intensity and load creates positive results through the additional overload on the muscular system.

Understand that you place greater loads on your body with this technique. Because of this fact, be sure to adjust your recovery time accordingly.

The following examples should help you understand the superset:

- Superset using two exercises for the same body part: biceps barbell curls supersetted with seated biceps dumbbell curls; 3 sets × 10 repetitions; no rest between exercises.
- Superset using exercises for opposing agonist and antagonist muscles—biceps cable curls supersetted with triceps cable extensions; 3 sets × 10 repetitions; no rest between exercises.

Tri-Sets

Another principle of advanced training programs is the tri-set. For a tri-set, you alternate between three exercises in a row, then repeat the circuit. Like a superset, a tri-set can involve a single body part or three separate body parts. The theory behind tri-sets is similar to supersets—increase the intensity of the resistance program by increasing the load and volume while decreasing the recovery time between exercises. Here are two examples of tri-sets:

- Tri-set using three exercises for the same body part: biceps barbell curls, seated biceps dumbbell curls, and hammer curls; 3 sets × 10 repetitions; no rest between exercises.
- Tri-set using three exercises for three different body parts: wide-grip chins, flat-bench flys, and seated dumbbell shoulder press; 3 sets × 10 repetitions; no rest between exercises.

Pyramiding

The final advanced training principle we will discuss is pyramiding, which is similar to cycling but goes a step further. It involves multiple sets of a single exercise, with an increase in weight before each set for a predetermined number of sets. Once you have completed the number of sets, increasing the weight per set, you decrease the weight per set for a predetermined number of sets. The idea is to increase the total volume you lift within a specific training session. Table 10.3 shows how pyramiding is introduced for a bench press.

Sample Program

You are now familiar with a group of training principles that will benefit both your resistance training and martial arts endeavors. Remember that at this point your training is cross-specific to your martial art and individual needs.

Following is an example of an intermediate training program geared toward developing muscular strength for judo. The training principles used in this program are split system, cycling, multiple sets, and

Table 10.3   Sample Pyramid Program for a Bench Press

Set	Repetitions	Load
1	12	165
2	10	190
3	8	220
4	10	185
5	12	155

repetition variation. The first program outline details the workouts for Monday, Wednesday, and Friday. The second program outline details the workouts for Tuesday, Thursday, and Saturday. On Sunday, the focus is on rest and recovery.

This sample intermediate training program is geared toward the development of muscular strength. It covers a seven-day period. You can follow the sample setup and guidelines until you achieve an advanced training level. Remember to gear your program to the specific requirements of your martial art and your personal goals. If you do not see any positive results after training for a couple of weeks at an intermediate level, modify the program to fit your fitness level, martial arts discipline, and goals.

An important point to remember is that each person is unique, and your training program needs to be tailored to your specific needs. There is no "cookie cutter" program that can give everyone the results they set out to reach. You will get better over time as you learn how your body responds to resistance training. Then you will be able to change exercises, intensity levels, and other variables to keep you going in the right direction.

Keep these points in mind as you develop and progress through the intermediate program. Use the information in this book to individualize your program to achieve the goals you have set up.

Monday, Wednesday, Friday Workout

Program Outline

1. Warm-up
2. Flexibility exercises (chapter 3)
3. Torso-stabilization exercises (chapter 5)
4. Joint-stabilization exercises (chapter 4)
5. Core exercises (chapter 6)
6. Anaerobic training (chapter 8)

Flexibility Exercises

1. Calf Stretch
2. Seated Groin Stretch
3. Straddle Groin Stretch
4. Thigh Lunge
5. Side Lunge Stretch
6. Side Quad Flex
7. Single-Arm Side Bend

8. Supermans (Alternating Arms)

9. Back Flexion

10. Back Extension

11. Neck Side to Side

12. Arm Cross

13. Arm Flexion

Torso-Stabilization Exercises

1. Low Back Press

2. Single-Leg Low Back Raise

3. Balanced Back Extension

4. Supermans (Both Arms)

5. Medicine Ball Abdominal Crunches

6. Abdominal Side Crunches

Joint-Stabilization Exercises

1. Butt-Ups

2. Flex-T Push-Ups

3. One-Arm Side-Ups

4. Shoulder Circles

5. Hitchhikers

6. Triceps Extensions

7. Internal Rotation

8. External Rotation

9. Reverse Rotators

10. Dumbbell Crosses

11. Flex-T Rotators

12. Upright Flys

13. Butterflies

14. Bent-Over Pulls

15. Bent-Over Flys

Core Exercises

1. Power Clean

2. Push Press

3. Squat

    4. Deadlift

    5. Biceps Barbell Curl

    6. Triceps Cable Extension

Anaerobic Training

    1. Interval Sprints (2 times per week)

    2. Hill Sprints

Tuesday, Thursday, Saturday

Program Outline

    1. Warm-up

    2. Flexibility exercises (chapter 3)

    3. Judo training

    4. Torso-stabilization exercises (chapter 5)

    5. Joint-stabilization exercises (chapter 4)

    6. Aerobic training (chapter 8)

Flexibility Exercises

    1. Calf Stretch

    2. Seated Groin Stretch

    3. Straddle Groin Stretch

    4. Thigh Lunge

    5. Side Lunge Stretch

    6. Side Quad Flex

    7. Single-Arm Side Bend

    8. Supermans (Alternating Arms)

    9. Back Flexion

  10. Back Extension

  11. Neck Side to Side

  12. Arm Cross

  13. Arm Flexion

Torso-Stabilization Exercises

    1. Low Back Press

    2. Single-Leg Low Back Raise

3. Abdominal Crunches

4. Abdominal Side Crunches

Joint-Stabilization Exercises

1. Butt-Ups

2. Flex-T Push-Ups

3. One-Arm Side-Ups

4. Shoulder Circles

5. Hitchhikers

6. Triceps Extensions

7. Internal Rotation

8. External Rotation

9. Reverse Rotators

Aerobic Training

Ride a stationary bicycle for 25 minutes.

ADVANCED TRAINING PROGRAM

The advanced training program can be developed in the same way as the intermediate program. The advanced program also is specific to the requirements of your martial art and individualized goals. You should implement a periodization schedule around tournaments or upcoming martial art events. Principles introduced in the intermediate program (split system, heavy-light system, cycling) will be used. The greatest difference between the intermediate and advanced programs is the increased volume, load, frequency, and intensity of the program. The advanced training programs presented here are only sample programs, so use them as guides. You must design a program specific to your martial art and personal goals.

People with approximately six months of training experience should look to begin training with an advanced program. Before you begin this phase of training, be completely comfortable with all the principles introduced in the intermediate program. Before mapping out your program, it is a good idea to review the information in previous chapters.

Remember to be goal-specific in the layout of your program, and train specific to your art. For example, if you participate in taekwondo, which requires extensive muscular endurance and power, you should focus your training around these requirements. Someone involved in judo would train around muscular strength and power rather than endurance. Use the principles described in previous chapters to tailor your advanced program to your goals. Begin with a needs analysis, set up your goals, review the biomechanics of your martial art, and develop a program that allows you to meet your goals.

At this level, you should develop your training around a periodization schedule that includes different phases. (For more information on periodization, see page 154.) Remember that you may synchronize your training with a competitive event or in accordance with specific goals. Set up your program with a periodization schedule that includes a 6- to 12-month block of time. Establish the different phases of your schedule with distinct goals to be achieved by the end of each phase. For example, in the first phase of a 12-month periodization schedule, you decide to increase muscular endurance. You plan your training to increase muscular endurance and set a time frame to achieve it. Your periodization schedule can also revolve around a martial arts tournament or belt test.

Use the following sample programs when developing your own advanced program. The advanced training programs follow the same exercise order as intermediate programs. The only addition is plyometrics.

Two sample programs are included. The first program is geared toward the development of muscular endurance. This program is ideal for a person practicing muay thai who is focusing on developing greater stamina. The second program is geared toward the development of muscular power. This program is excellent for a person in karate focusing on developing greater punching and kicking power. The only new principles in these programs are the systematic use of supersets (two exercises for the same body part), pyramids (increased weight for each set for a specific exercise), and tri-sets (three exercises for the same body part).

Advanced Training Program to Develop Muscular Endurance

This program focuses on developing muscular endurance and would be a good training program for a martial artist practicing muay thai who wants to develop better stamina. High repetitions—12 or more per set—of each exercise will help the martial artist develop endurance.

Monday, Thursday, Saturday Workout

Program Outline

1. Warm-up
2. Flexibility exercises (chapter 3)

3. Torso-stabilization exercises (chapter 5)

4. Joint-stabilization exercises (chapter 4)

5. Core exercises (chapter 6)

6. Anaerobic training (chapter 8)

7. Plyometrics (chapter 7) (no plyometrics on Saturday)

Flexibility Exercises

1. Calf Stretch

2. Seated Groin Stretch

3. Straddle Groin Stretch

4. Thigh Lunge

5. Side Lunge Stretch

6. Side Quad Flex

7. Single-Arm Side Bend

8. Supermans (Alternating Arms)

9. Back Flexion

10. Back Extension

11. Neck Side to Side

12. Arm Cross

13. Arm Flexion

Torso-Stabilization Exercises

1. Low Back Press

2. Single-Leg Low Back Raise

3. Balanced Back Extension

4. Supermans (Both Arms)

5. Abdominal Crunches

6. Abdominal Side Crunches

7. Physio Ball Low Back Extensions

8. Physio Ball Crunches

9. Physio Ball Rotations

10. Physio Ball Jack Knife

Joint-Stabilization Exercises

1. Butt-Ups

2. Flex-T Push-Ups

3. One-Arm Side-Ups

4. Shoulder Circles

5. Hitchhikers

6. Triceps Extensions

7. Internal Rotation

8. External Rotation

9. Reverse Rotators

10. Dumbbell Crosses

11. Flex-T Rotators

12. Upright Flys

13. Butterflies

14. Bent-Over Pulls

15. Bent-Over Flys

Core Exercises

1. Dumbbell Bench Press

2. Bent-Over Barbell Row

3. Wide Grip Chin

4. Biceps Barbell Curl

5. Reverse Biceps Barbell Curl

6. Triceps Cable Extension

7. Lunges

8. Medicine Ball Skater

9. Leg Curl

10. Standing Calf Raise

Anaerobic Training

1. Interval Sprints

2. Cone Zig-Zag

3. Four-Corner Carioca Drill

Plyometrics (Monday and Thursday Only)

1. Medicine Ball Push-Up

2. Kneeling Medicine Ball Throw

3. Medicine Ball Overhead Throw

Tuesday, Friday Workout

Program Outline

1. Warm-up
2. Flexibility exercises (chapter 3)
3. Torso-stabilization exercises (chapter 5)
4. Joint-stabilization exercises (chapter 4)
5. Muay thai training
6. Plyometrics (chapter 7)
7. Aerobic training (chapter 8)

Flexibility Exercises

1. Calf Stretch
2. Seated Groin Stretch
3. Straddle Groin Stretch
4. Thigh Lunge
5. Side Lunge Stretch
6. Side Quad Flex
7. Single-Arm Side Bend
8. Supermans (Alternating Arms)
9. Back Flexion
10. Back Extension
11. Neck Side to Side
12. Arm Cross
13. Arm Flexion

Torso-Stabilization Exercises

1. Low Back Press
2. Single-Leg Low Back Raise
3. Balanced Back Extension
4. Supermans (Both Arms)
5. Abdominal Crunches
6. Abdominal Side Crunches

Joint-Stabilization Exercises

1. Butt-Ups
2. Flex-T Push-Ups

3. One-Arm Side-Ups

4. Shoulder Circles

5. Hitchhikers

6. Triceps Extensions

7. Internal Rotation

8. External Rotation

9. Reverse Rotators

Plyometrics

1. Split Squat Jumps

2. Double-Leg Tuck Jump

3. Lateral Cone Hop

Aerobic Training

Ride a stationary bicycle for 20 minutes.

Wednesday Workout

Program Outline

1. Warm-up

2. Flexibility exercises (chapter 3)

3. Torso-stabilization exercises (chapter 5)

4. Joint-stabilization exercises (chapter 4)

Flexibility Exercises

1. Calf Stretch

2. Seated Groin Stretch

3. Straddle Groin Stretch

4. Thigh Lunge

5. Side Lunge Stretch

6. Side Quad Flex

7. Single-Arm Side Bend

8. Supermans (Alternating Arms)

9. Back Flexion

10. Back Extension

11. Neck Side to Side

12. Arm Cross

13. Arm Flexion

Torso-Stabilization Exercises

1. Low Back Press

2. Single-Leg Low Back Raise

3. Balanced Back Extension

4. Supermans (Both Arms)

5. Abdominal Crunches

6. Abdominal Side Crunches

Joint-Stabilization Exercises

1. Butt-Ups

2. Flex-T Push-Ups

3. One-Arm Side-Ups

4. Shoulder Circles

5. Hitchhikers

6. Triceps Extensions

7. Internal Rotation

8. External Rotation

9. Reverse Rotators

Advanced Training Program to Develop Muscular Power

This program focuses on developing muscular power and would be a good program for a martial artist in karate who wants to develop better punching and kicking power.

Monday, Wednesday, Friday Workout

Program Outline

1. Warm-up

2. Flexibility exercises (chapter 3)

3. Torso-stabilization exercises (chapter 5)

4. Joint-stabilization exercises (chapter 4)

   5. Core exercises (chapter 6)

   6. Anaerobic training (chapter 8)

   7. Plyometrics (chapter 7) (no plyometrics on Wednesday)

Flexibility Exercises

   1. Calf Stretch

   2. Seated Groin Stretch

   3. Straddle Groin Stretch

   4. Thigh Lunge

   5. Side Lunge Stretch

   6. Side Quad Flex

   7. Single-Arm Side Bend

   8. Supermans (Alternating Arms)

   9. Back Flexion

   10. Back Extension

   11. Neck Side to Side

   12. Arm Cross

   13. Arm Flexion

Torso-Stabilization Exercises

   1. Low Back Press

   2. Single-Leg Low Back Raise

   3. Balanced Back Extension

   4. Supermans (Both Arms)

   5. Abdominal Crunches

   6. Abdominal Side Crunches

   7. Physio Ball Low Back Extensions

   8. Physio Ball Crunches

   9. Physio Ball Rotations

   10. Physio Ball Jack Knife

Joint-Stabilization Exercises

   1. Butt-Ups

   2. Flex-T Push-Ups

3. One-Arm Side-Ups

4. Shoulder Circles

5. Hitchhikers

6. Triceps Extensions

7. Internal Rotation

8. External Rotation

9. Reverse Rotators

10. Dumbbell Crosses

11. Flex-T Rotators

12. Upright Flys

13. Butterflies

14. Bent-Over Pulls

15. Bent-Over Flys

Core Exercises

1. Power Clean

2. Squat

3. Deadlift

4. Dumbbell Bench Press

5. Biceps Barbell Curl

6. Triceps Cable Extension

7. Standing Calf Raise

Anaerobic Training

1. Sprint/Jog Intervals

2. Hill Sprints

Plyometrics (Monday and Friday Only)

1. Double-Leg Tuck Jump

2. Split Squat Jumps

3. In-Depth Push-Up

4. Kneeling Medicine Ball Throw

5. Medicine Ball Overhead Throw

Tuesday, Thursday, Saturday Workout

Program Outline

1. Warm-up
2. Flexibility exercises (chapter 3)
3. Torso-stabilization exercises (chapter 5)
4. Joint-stabilization exercises (chapter 4)
5. Karate training
6. Aerobic training (chapter 8)

Flexibility Exercises

1. Calf Stretch
2. Seated Groin Stretch
3. Straddle Groin Stretch
4. Thigh Lunge
5. Side Lunge Stretch
6. Side Quad Flex
7. Single-Arm Side Bend
8. Supermans (Alternating Arms)
9. Back Flexion
10. Back Extension
11. Neck Side to Side
12. Arm Cross
13. Arm Flexion

Torso-Stabilization Exercises

1. Low Back Press
2. Single-Leg Low Back Raise
3. Balanced Back Extension
4. Supermans (Both Arms)
5. Abdominal Crunches
6. Abdominal Side Crunches

Joint-Stabilization Exercises

1. Butt-Ups
2. Flex-T Push-Ups
3. One-Arm Side-Ups
4. Shoulder Circles
5. Hitchhikers
6. Triceps Extensions
7. Internal Rotation
8. External Rotation
9. Reverse Rotators

Aerobic Training

Jog on a treadmill for 20 minutes.

SUMMARY

In the final chapter of this book, you have learned a lot of information to help you complete your cross training for your martial art. Remember to use the sample programs as examples of how to develop your own individualized training program. Proceed at your own pace through the development of your training program. Olympians are not made in one day.

Use all the information provided in this book for your benefit. Break down the physical requirements of your martial art and develop your program from that point. Keep in mind the importance of rest, recovery, and proper nutrition in the development of your mind, body, and spirit as you grow in your martial art. Training smart achieves more than just training hard. Keep this thought in mind: "Every long journey begins with one small step." Thank you for giving me the opportunity to help you on your journey. Best of luck.

ABOUT THE AUTHOR

Sean M. Cochran, a second-degree black belt in taekwondo and NSCA-certified strength and conditioning specialist, has served as a consultant for many professional baseball clubs, collegiate athletic organizations, and professional athletes from a wide variety of sports. He currently serves as the minor league strength and conditioning coordinator for the San Diego Padres baseball organization.

Cochran is a member of the American College of Sports Medicine and is certified by the National Strength and Conditioning Association and the Chiropractic Rehabilitation Association. He is the conditioning coordinator for the Human Performance Group, which develops conditioning programs for both the public and for athletes. Cochran is also a member of the USA Weightlifting Federation, and he coaches on the club level. He has been involved in several fitness videos and coauthored *Stronger Arms and Upper Body* with Tom House (Human Kinetics, 2000). Cochran lives in San Diego, California.